Quick to Make

Stylish Gifts to Craft in a Day

The Editors of Threads

The Taunton Press

The Taunton Press
Inspiration for hands-on living™

The Taunton Press, Inc., 63 South Main Street, PO Box 5506, Newtown, CT 06470-5506
e-mail: tp@taunton.com

Distributed by Publishers Group West

JACKET/COVER DESIGNER: CAROL SINGER
INTERIOR DESIGNER: SUSAN FAZEKAS
LAYOUT ARTIST: SUSAN FAZEKAS
FRONT COVER PHOTOGRAPHERS: JUDI RUTZ, © THE TAUNTON PRESS, INC. (TOP LEFT); SLOAN HOWARD, © THE
TAUNTON PRESS, INC. (TOP RIGHT); SCOTT PHILLIPS, © THE TAUNTON PRESS, INC. (BOTTOM LEFT); SLOAN
HOWARD, © SLOAN HOWARD (BOTTOM RIGHT)
BACK COVER PHOTOGRAPHERS: SCOTT PHILLIPS, © THE TAUNTON PRESS, INC. (TOP); SLOAN HOWARD, © THE
TAUNTON PRESS, INC. (BOTTOM)

LIBRARY OF CONGRESS CATALOGING-IN-PUBLICATION DATA
Quick to make : stylish gifts to craft in a day / the editors of Threads.
        p. cm.
    ISBN 1-56158-513-0
      1. Textile crafts. 2. Wearable art. I. Threads (Newtown, Conn.)

TT699 .Q53 2002
745.5–dc21   2001057376

Printed in the United States of America
10 9 8 7 6 5 4 3 2 1

Contributors

Denise Alborn
Button-Up Spreads and Throws, p. 81
Denise Alborn and her mother, Rita Alborn, own Fifth Ave. Fabric & Clothing Gallery, in Olympia, WA, where they create original designs and sell natural-fiber fabrics.

Susan B. Allen
Overstitched Bags and Portfolios, p. 58
Susan B. Allen is a contributing editor of *Threads* magazine. Her clothing and accessories designs are sold across the United States under the Susan Allen Art label.

Christine M. Anderson
Needlebooks for Hand-Stitchers, p. 84
Christine Anderson is a needle artist, writer, and lecturer in San Francisco, CA. Her work has been exhibited in numerous shows nationwide.

Judy Atwell
Seashells to Wear, p. 42
Judy Atwell of Aptos, CA, designs, teaches, and writes about crafts, jewelry, and wearable art.

Debra Blum and Moises Diaz
Call 'em Irresistible—Beads and Tulle, p. 34
Gossamer Ribbon-Work Scarves, p. 37
Debra Blum and Moises Diaz form the New York City design team Debra Moises.

Shirley Botsford
A Pillow from Neckties, p. 70
Shirley Botsford, author of *Daddy's Ties* (Krause Publications), teaches and lectures about design and all areas of needlework for quilt guilds and sewing organizations. She teaches draping and industry-related courses at Marist College in Poughkeepsie, NY.

Annie Coan
Old-World Treasures: Clay Buttons and Jewelry, p. 16
Annie Coan's techniques are published in books and magazines. She is an art education curator and teaching artist with a specialty in fiber arts and polymer clay.

Jane Conlon
Gorgeous Beaded Buttons: Make Just One or a Set, p. 18
Pillow and Pyramid Gift Boxes, p. 67
Jane Conlon teaches sewing and embellishment techniques at 27th Street Fabrics in Eugene, OR. She is a frequent contributor to *Threads* magazine and the author of *Fine Embellishment Techniques* (The Taunton Press).

Ingrid Fraley
The Saturn Hatpin, p. 6
Ingrid Fraley is a former principal dancer with the Joffrey Ballet and the American Ballet Theatre. She is currently an actor living in New York City.

Wanda Gayer
Dimensional Embroidery, p. 27
Wanda Gayer has taught Brazilian embroidery and silk ribbon design for 10 years. She created the machine-embroidered foliage in her article on her Brother® Pacesetter® Embroidery Machine at her sewing-machine shop in Downey, CA.

Mary Jo Hiney
Stamped Fabric Is Only the Beginning, p. 22
Take the Ribbon Road, p. 30
Embroidered Felt Trivets, p. 64
Mary Jo Hiney of Los Osos, CA, is a designer and author of 11 books on decorative accessories for the home (all published by Sterling).

Louise LoPinto Hutchison
Fold a Fabric-Origami Treasure Box, p. 78
Louise LoPinto Hutchison is a graphic designer, writer, and teacher. A quilter for the past 15 years, she is a member of the Warwick Valley Quilters' Guild in Warwick, NY.

Therese M. Inverso
Patchwork Puzzle Pins, p. 11
Therese M. Inverso teaches knitting and makes felted wool originals in Haddon Township, NJ.

Linda Lee
Great Pillows 1,2,3, p. 72
Ribbonwork Holiday Stocking, p. 76
Linda Lee is the owner of The Sewing Workshop in San Francisco. She is a contributing editor to *Threads* magazine and the sewing expert on *Our Place* on HGTV. Her books include *Sewing Edges and Corners* and *Sewing Stylish Home Projects* (The Taunton Press) *and Simply Slipcovers* and *Simply Pillows* (Sunset Books).

Connie Long
Stitch an Easy Bra-Slip, p. 40
Connie Long teaches sewing classes and is the author of *Easy Guide to Sewing Blouses, Easy Guide to Sewing Linings, Sewing with Knits,* and *Embellish Chic: Detailing Ready-to-Wear,* all published by The Taunton Press.

Anna Mazur
Customized Hangers, p. 87
Anna Mazur is President of the Connecticut Chapter of the American Sewing Guild. She is an award-winning designer and lecturer. She has also been a featured guest on HGTV's *Sew Much More.*

Sally McCann
Pincushions with Personality, p. 89
Sally McCann teaches fitting, sewing, and pattern-drafting in Baltimore, MD. She is the author of *Every Sewer's Guide to the Perfect Fit* (Lark Books).

Karen Morris
Your Very Own Dévoré Velvet, p. 24
Two Sew-Easy Scarves, p. 48
Wrap Yourself in Soutache, p. 50
The Simplest Summer Skirt, p. 60
A contributing editor of *Threads* magazine, Karen Morris works as a freelance writer and designer. She is the author of *Sewing Lingerie that Fits* (The Taunton Press) and has designed her own line of hand-loomed knitwear.

Nancy Nehring
Easy Braided Belts, p. 44
Nancy Nehring is an author, teacher, and designer in the needle arts field. She is the author of three books: *50 Heirloom Buttons to Make, The Lacy Knitting of Mary Schiffmann,* and *Ribbon Trims.* She has designed for DMC, Donna Karan, and Better Homes and Gardens. She is the education co-chair for the Crochet Guild of America.

Marlene O'Tousa
From Buttons to Bracelets, p. 8
With 35 years of sewing experience, Marlene teaches at G Street Fabrics in Rockville, MD. She has also added one-of-a-kind jewelry design to her repertoire of skills and teaching credits.

Laura "Roxy" White
Fabric Cuff Bracelets, p. 14
Stitch a Pie Bag, p. 55
Variations on a Shrug, p. 52
A former associate editor at *Threads* magazine, Roxy is currently studying doll making and designing clothes patterns.

Contents

Introduction

*m*any of us would love to make hand-crafted gifts for family and friends or small luxury items for ourselves, but we just can't find the time. This collection of 31 "Quick to Make" articles from *Threads* magazine solves the time dilemma and proves that sophisticated and stylish gifts don't have to be difficult or time consuming.

From jewelry and clothing to home dec and embellishment ideas, you'll find a variety of projects for everyone on your gift list. If you sew, many of these projects can be made from leftover scraps. If you don't, the materials can be easily purchased at a fabric or craft store or refer to the Resources section in the back of the book. You might even want to gather up a group of friends for an afternoon of social creativity. You can swap scraps and be inspired by one another— besides, working together is fun.

We encourage you to think of these projects as a springboard from which to create your own designs. With a bit of imagination, you can adapt these ideas and techniques in nearly endless ways. And whether you make the projects as shown or in some variation of your own, you may want to make two or more of each—some to give away and one to keep for yourself. This won't take you long because all of these gifts are truly quick to make. ●

If you love jewelry and other finishing touches, we invite you to craft pieces that reflect your personal style. "Antiqued" jewelry is simple to make and the designs are endless. Know someone who loves puzzles? Give her an unusual puzzle pin made from fabric scraps. Or turn your scraps into a smart cuff bracelet. And don't overlook all those stray buttons in your sewing box—make them into stylish bracelets. Speaking of buttons—why not create a beautiful set of one-of-a-kind beaded buttons? Use them to transform a simple sweater or to adorn a wrapped gift for someone who sews. ●

part 1

Buttons, Bracelets, and Pins

The Saturn Hatpin:
Quickly Sew a Beaded Pin for Your Lapel or Chapeau

*h*ere's an intriguing hatpin shape that I call, for obvious reasons, the Saturn pin. It's fun to make and wear, especially if you use a gorgeous fabric. This nifty pin can be used to anchor a hat, and it also looks beautiful used as a stickpin to fasten a scarf or decorate a lapel or beret.

GATHER A FEW INGREDIENTS

My original Saturn pin was constructed with a cork ball as the core, but these balls have become hard to find of late. So my new version of this hatpin incorporates a child's bouncy ball, which works quite well and which you can find at any toy store. You can use a ¾-in.- to 1-in.-diameter ball.

The pin doesn't require much fabric, so choose something ultraluxurious. Dig out those tiny remnants of silk matelasse, satin, taffeta, dupioni, or hammered silk to create a beautiful pin.

You'll need a 5-in.-long, balltop hatpin base and clutch. The base of a hatpin resembles a long straight pin with or without a flat or ball head. The clutch shields the

A balltop hatpin base makes this pin more stable. A child's bouncy ball forms its inner structure.

pin's sharp point. Both are available from sources that sell jewelry findings.

You'll also need seed beads; about 2 yd. of thin rattail cord to cover the ball; thin, sturdy cardboard such as the back of a writing pad; a fabric glue such as Magnatac 809 by Beacon Chemical; and an all-purpose jewelry glue like Eclectic Products' E-6000™ or Bond 527. For cutting the ball and cardboard, you'll need a craft knife.

A FEW NOTES ABOUT CONSTRUCTION

If you can't find a balltop hatpin base, you can easily make one by sliding a ½-in.-diameter (12mm) bead or fake pearl onto a plain base and securing it at the top with all-purpose glue. This gives a more stable surface on which to glue the bouncy ball.

The hardest part about making this hatpin is cutting the bouncy ball without cutting your finger. Use a fine-point marker to draw a line around the center of the ball, unless your ball has a seam you can follow, as mine did. Draw a line perpendicular to this centerline, which you'll use later to line up the halves for reassembly. With the craft knife, carefully slice the ball in half. Now follow the step-by-step instructions on the facing page. In no time, you'll have a great hatpin to wear or give as a unique gift. ●

A balltop hatpin base makes this pin more stable. A child's bouncy ball forms its inner structure.

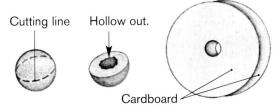

Cutting line   Hollow out.

Cardboard

STEP 1. Cut bouncy ball in half at center. Hollow out each half so the ball top of your hatpin base fits easily inside. For a ¾-in. bouncy ball, cut two cardboard circles 1 ¾ in. in diameter. (For a 1-in. ball, cut the circles 2 in. in diameter.) Mark and cut a hole in the center of each circle to fit the top of the hatpin base.

STEP 2. Cut two fabric circles ½ in. larger in diameter than the cardboard. Starting with one fabric circle, sew running stitch ⅛ in. from cut edge of fabric. Pull thread to draw fabric tight over cardboard; glue lightly under edge of fabric, and tie off. Slash fabric over hole, from center out. Place glue on circle's inside edge, push fabric through hole, and smooth over edge. Repeat.

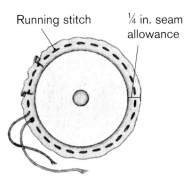

Running stitch   ¼ in. seam allowance

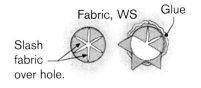

Fabric, WS   Glue

Slash fabric over hole.

STEP 3. Glue wrong sides of circles together, and clamp with clothespins to dry.

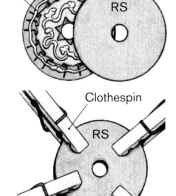

Glue

RS

Clothespin

RS

STEP 4. To assemble pin, glue hatpin base into half of bouncy ball, with pin sticking through center, as shown. Let dry. Apply glue to flat face of both ball halves; place fabric-covered circles over hatpin base, and top with remaining ball half. Press firmly together. Let dry.

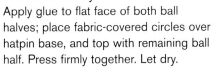

STEP 5. Cut rattail in half. Place glue on half of ball. Wrap with cord, starting from outside. Continue to center. Cut cord, leaving end to tuck under last spiral with pin. Dry. Repeat on other side.

STEP 6. Sew beads around edge of fabric circle, using stitch below. Sew three to five beads at top center of ball.

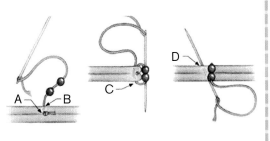

A   B   C   D

From Buttons to Bracelets

There's more than one way to attach buttons: String safety pins on elastic cord for shank buttons (below left). Make shanks from pearl cotton for buttons with holes (above right), or sew buttons directly onto elastic and add dangling button charms (below right).

*d*o you love buttons? Collect them madly and impulsively like I do? If so, you'll enjoy showing them off with these attention-grabbing bracelets. You do need lots of buttons—about 150, more or less. (If you don't have enough, here's a perfect excuse to acquire more.) Buttons come in such variety that you can make a bracelet that's elegant, funky, or subtle, depending on the buttons' style and the way you combine them.

LET THE BUTTONS INSPIRE

First choose the buttons for your bracelet. When I'm designing one, I look for buttons in my collection that have something in common. For example, I used only silver-colored buttons for the bracelet on the model's right arm. Sticking to a single color focuses the bracelet's design on the shine and texture of the different buttons. Color is also the theme that unites the buttons in the mostly red bracelet shown at left and the shell button bracelet shown above. I used different colors on the bracelet shown below right, but chose buttons with a common personality; a few are Bakelite buttons, and the rest are inspired from the colors and shapes of that era. Sometimes fewer, larger buttons make a strong design, like those on the model's left arm.

EASY ASSEMBLY

Once you've gathered a pile of buttons you like, it's time to arrange them into a button work of art. I've used several different approaches with these bracelets, but they all use elastic cord to form the foundation on which to attach the buttons. (The elastic ensures a snug fit, but it is easy to remove from your wrist and eliminates the need for a clasp.)

Safety-pin bracelet

One method involves stringing about 150 safety pins onto round elastic cord (either black or white, depending on the colors of the buttons) and fastening a button to each pin (see the sidebar "Secure Buttons to Elastic" on p. 10). If you want to use safety pins in a color other than silver or gold, you'll find it's easy to spray-paint them.

You won't need much elastic cord; a yard makes three or four bracelets. Cut an 8-in. to 12-in. length of cord, and tape one end to a work surface. String all 150 safety pins onto the cord, going through the hole at the end of each pin. Now tie the cord snugly around your wrist with a square knot, which won't come loose. Pull tight, and leave 1 in. to 2 in. of the elastic's ends—they'll disappear into the mass of buttons.

It's easiest to use buttons with shanks rather than holes, but if you do want to include buttons with holes, make a thread shank for them on the sewing machine, following the directions in the sidebar below.

Thread-tie bracelet

The shell button bracelet is also made by stringing together lots of buttons on an elastic cord, but I've omitted the safety pins. Instead I made simple shanks from pearl cotton. I strung the buttons onto the cord and then tied it to fit my wrist.

Why save buttons for garments only? With a little elastic cord, some safety pins, and an abundance of buttons, you can make an easy bracelet that's fun or downright dramatic.

Quick Tip

Here's an easy way to make thread shanks for buttons with holes. Set your machine for zigzag stitches, place the button right side up on a piece of tear-away stabilizer, and center it under the machine's needle. Lower the presser foot onto the button. Now drop the feed dogs (very important), loosen the needle tension to about one or two, then use the handwheel to make sure the width of the zigzag stitch is the same as the holes in the button. Using the foot pedal, sew the button to the stabilizer. If you have many buttons needing thread shanks, sew them all onto the stabilizer before tearing it away.

Spray-paint safety pins any color you want. Stick the pins into a piece of cardboard, then spray them from the top and all four sides.

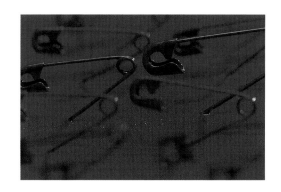

Quick Tip

For a really plump bracelet, I sometimes attach two smaller buttons to the same safety pin, or I attach an additional safety pin to one on the cord and add another button or two to that one. This gives me a really jingly-jangly display of my beloved buttons.

Sew-on bracelet

I used a different method for the bracelet shown at bottom right on p. 8. Instead of round elastic cord, I used ¼-in. flat elastic, sewing the ends together securely with a zigzag stitch. I stitched the larger buttons with holes directly onto the elastic. I thought this would produce a flatter bracelet, but I found that as the buttons curved around my wrist, the elastic showed unattractively. The solution? I tied smaller buttons between the larger ones to fill in the gaps, stacking them together and letting them dangle like charms. So much for making a quieter bracelet! These buttons want to announce their arrival.

I'm collecting black and gold buttons for an outrageous, over-the-top rhinestone-button bracelet. I'm also considering one made entirely of buttons featuring fruit. So what's in your button box? ●

Secure Buttons to Elastic

Safety-Pin Button Bracelet

String safety pins on elastic cord, tie square knot in cord, and slide button onto safety pin. Build a thicker bracelet by attaching more safety pins to original ones.

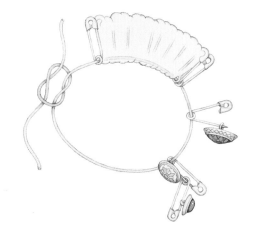

A Variety of Ties

To make a bracelet from buttons with holes instead of shanks, use string, pearl cotton, ribbon, yarn, or heavy thread to tie them on the elastic. Make them as close to the elastic as you want, or let them dangle.

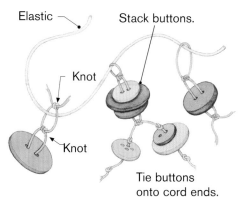

Elastic

Stack buttons.

Knot

Knot

Tie buttons onto cord ends.

Patchwork Puzzle Pins

*i*magine creating quick, small works of art that combine elements of strip piecing and random patchwork techniques. And the best part is that you can wear them!

My little lapel pins are so easy to make because, using felted wool, you need no seam allowances—you just butt the edges together and sew. But what you design while playing may surprise you. I'll suggest several ways to get started and you can take it from there.

The pins you see here are made from wool melton coating fabrics. But my favorite fabric for this patchwork is the thin felted wool I create from thrift-shop sweaters made of lambswool or lambswool blends (see Resources on p. 91 for wool felt sources). You can even use your own handmade felt to make these pins, as long as it's fairly thin.

If you want to use melton cloth, hold the fabric up to the light before buying it; if it's thin enough to see through, you'll need to felt the fabric in a hot machine-wash-and-

dry cycle and press it before sewing. Thicker melton cloth can be cut and sewn without preparation.

Although melton has a nap, you don't need to maintain the nap direction when piecing. Light playing on the nap as it falls in different directions creates a rich fabric.

HOW TO PIECE THE PATCHWORK

Basically, the patchwork process involves repeatedly slicing and joining sections of fabric to get an effect you like. I follow only two rules: First, I never (ever!) measure, which adds a random element to the patchwork and makes the work easier and more fun. Second, I sew continuously from one pair of fabrics to the next, which keeps the presser foot at the same level and allows each new seam to begin at the very beginning. It also saves a lot of thread.

Quick sewing details

An open-toe appliqué foot allows you to see exactly where you're sewing, although an ordinary presser foot will do. For the stitching, use a size 80/12 needle; a multiple zigzag stitch 3 mm to 4 mm wide and 0.5 mm long;

Multiple Zigzag

The machine stitch below is great
for joining felted patchwork.

Widen and shorten stitch
for a firm grasp on each
abutted fabric edge.

and fine, 0.004 monofilament nylon thread
for the upper and lower thread. I use clear
monofilament most of the time and switch
to the smoke thread only for all-dark colors.
Because fine monofilament thread sometimes slips in the bobbin case, I reserve a
special case, with the screw tightened, for
sewing with this thread.

Abutted seams

To join two pieces of wool, simply butt the
edges firmly together as they pass under the
presser foot. As you complete each seam,
hold it up to the light to check that the
edges are tight; if light shows through, cut

the seam apart and resew it. Faulty seams
won't stand up to repeated slicing and sewing.
Finally, iron the patchwork frequently, using a
press cloth and a steam iron set between wool
and cotton. Cutting and sewing felted wool
produces a lot of dust, so brush out the bobbin area of your machine and vacuum your
work area daily. You might also want to wear
a surgical mask while cutting and sewing to
avoid irritation.

A DESIGN NOTEBOOK

The ½-in.-wide striped fabric (shown top left
at the bottom of the facing page) is a useful
patchwork building block (remember, no
measuring!). If you use unfelted melton
cloth, cut the strips on the lengthwise grain;
for felted wool, cut in any direction. Butt
and sew the strips together to make a striped
fabric. Then slice the striped block again
lengthwise and reassemble it into narrow
stripes, and then slice widthwise and reassemble into checks. Or slice the stripes diagonally, turn half the new strips upside
down to create chevrons, and reassemble.
Multicolored checks give a more random effect (see the sample top right on p. 11). The
photos on the top of the facing page show
what happens when you use three- and four-
color stripes, then assemble narrow strips in
different ways. And the fabric shown at left
is simple to make, using wide and narrow
stripes that create a bold, graphic design.

Did I say this project was quick? In one
afternoon, I pieced enough patchwork wool
to make maybe a hundred pins. Of course,
framing and finishing them takes another day,
but the entire process is remarkably quick.

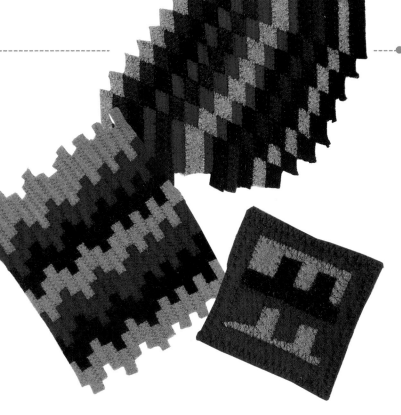

ON TO THE FINISHING

It's easy to transform a piece of patchwork into a finished pin. First, cut the patchwork into a square, rectangle, or trapezoid shape from ⅜ in. to 2¼ in. in either direction. Choose a color for the "frame," and stitch a strip to two sides, then frame the other two sides. Trim the frame to about ⅜ in. wide, and cut a larger piece for a backing from solid-color felted wool. To give the pin body, cut a piece of flat plastic (I use plastic milk bottles) about the size of the central patchwork. Stitch the framed top to the back, with the plastic piece floating inside. Finally, trim the edges of the back, without cutting into the stitching, and trim any stray thread ends.

To complete your pin, sew on a pin-back finding. And that's it! Make a pile of these pins for holiday gifts—each one will be unique. ●

Quick Tip

Instead of using plastic to give the pin body, use several layers of heavy-weight fusible interfacing.

Fabric Cuff Bracelets

Shape the contours of a cuff. Stephanie Kimura, of Jensen Beach, FL, layered thin cotton batting with tear-away stabilizer to embellish beautiful fabric for her cuffs. After removing the stabilizer, she created contours with satin stitches over the cuffs' tops, lining fabric, and a new piece of tear-away stabilizer.

While flipping through a magazine recently, a fabric cuff bracelet caught my eye, and it looked as easy to sew as a pillowcase. It was a simple rectangle of lined fabric, with fabric loop-and-button closures, and embellished with a splash of beads and stones. I looked at the price. Whoa!

I know sewers can easily create this fashion accessory, not only with more imagination and flair but also for a tenth of the price. To inspire you to try this fun project, I solicited sewn fabric cuffs from three designers and made a few myself. They're shown here with brief notes on how they were constructed.

FITTING THE WRIST

First you'll need to make a pattern for a fitted cuff. Measure the circumference of the wearer's wrist as well as the place on the arm where the cuff's upper edge will fall. If your cuff's design requires a snug fit so it won't rotate around the arm, use these two measurements to make a slight cone

Create a keepsake corsage-cuff, like this one stitched by Elizabeth Moir, of Mount Lawley, W.A., Australia. She nestled blooms made from wired taffeta and organza ribbon, velvet ribbon, beads, and a feather on a padded silk base.

Pay tribute to your favorite teachers. I needed only to browse through past issues of sewing magazines to find ideas for cuffs. I selected the techniques of Jeffrey Mayer and Todd Conover (slot seam) and Jean Liittschwager (corded pin-tucking) for my cuffs.

Basic Cuff Construction

Here's an easy approach to constructing a cuff: Cut fabric, using pattern made from your arm's measurements. Cut lining $\frac{1}{16}$ in. to $\frac{1}{8}$ in. shorter at each end (when sewn and turned, lining will pull cuff inward). After embellishing fabric, stitch fabric or elastic loop at one end as shown. Then place fabric and lining RSs together, and stitch around cuff, leaving one side section unsewn for turning. Trim seams and corners, then RS out sew opening closed, and attach buttons or beads to match loops.

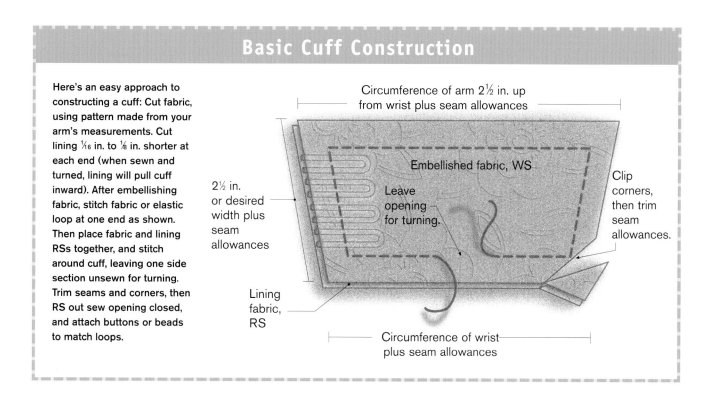

Circumference of arm 2½ in. up from wrist plus seam allowances

2½ in. or desired width plus seam allowances

Embellished fabric, WS

Leave opening for turning.

Clip corners, then trim seam allowances.

Lining fabric, RS

Circumference of wrist plus seam allowances

---

shape, which will conform to the arm and keep it from twisting around. Cylindrical shapes work well for many designs, too, but remember to use the measurement of the uppermost part of the arm. And don't forget to add seam allowances.

LET YOUR IMAGINATION TAKE OVER

Now, get out your favorite fabric scraps, ribbons, buttons, threads, and beads, and start playing. Cuffs can be constructed in any number of ways (one easy method is illustrated above). Keep in mind that soft, pliable lining feels nice against the skin, and plan closures so they can be easily opened and closed with one hand. Besides loop and button closures, consider snaps, hooks and eyes, ties, or Velcro®.

Custom cuffs are a natural addition to an outfit you've sewn, or make one for fun. As our designers' samples prove, there is no end to the effects and embellishments you can showcase on a cuff. ●

Feature a favorite button. Sandy Scrivano, of Sacramento, CA, focused on closures as embellishment for her cuffs. In the first example below, she cut soft suede leather with a rotary cutter fitted with shaped blades and punched holes to accommodate silk-ribbon stitches. In the next example (right), she glued leather strips to add dimension that complements a vintage belt buckle.

Old-World Treasures:
Clay Buttons and Jewelry

*d*o you love the look of ancient pottery, hand-carved ivory, and old bone? Using the very modern technique of photocopy transfer onto polymer clay, you can create timeworn-looking beauties to use as buttons and jewelry.

BROKEN POTTERY SHARDS

Using polymer clay, I like to create buttons and jewelry with the look of lost treasures, pieces that resemble weathered shards of pottery. By pressing photocopies onto the clay, I can easily transfer images from old photographs, drawings, or vintage laces. Photos and laces aren't damaged by the photocopier, so you can "borrow" designs without harming the originals.

First, adjust the copier

Play with the photocopier settings to get an image you like. Sometimes you can sharpen a fuzzy image by reducing it 25 to 50 percent. Adjusting the machine's light/dark setting can help you get an image with good contrast.

Mix and shape the clay

Mix various brands and shades of clay until you get an interesting color. After conditioning the clay by manipulating it with your hands for about ten minutes, you're ready to shape it. I roll it into a ⅛-in.-thick slab with a hand-crank pasta machine, but rolling the clay with a brayer (available at art-supply stores with linoleum-cutting materials) works as well. To produce an even width when hand-rolling, place a square chopstick on each side of the clay. I get a jagged, "pottery-shard" edge on a piece by pressing

the clay edge with a broken seashell. Or you can cut the clay with a knife or shears, or tiny cookie cutters.

Transfer a clear image

Cut or carefully rip the photocopy to the desired size—a ripped paper edge adds to the "discovered-treasure" effect. Place the paper, image-side down, on the thin slab of clay, and burnish, or rub, the aper gently with the back of a teaspoon. You can usually get a clear transfer in about 15 minutes. Lift a corner of the paper to check, then gently peel off the paper. If this doesn't work, cover the clay and inverted photocopy with a piece of scrap paper, weighting it with a heavy book, and leaving it in a warm spot such as on top of the VCR for about 24 hours.

Ready to bake and finish

Before baking, peel off the paper image. Mold the clay piece around a button form if you want a curved shape. To create a spot for a "jewel" in the finished piece, press it in place now, but remove it during baking. I use a toaster oven that I reserve for Fimo™ clay only. Lift the pieces off the work surface with a tissue

blade or thin knife, transfer to a baking sheet, and bake them in a preheated, 265-degree oven for one hour. Let the hot pieces cool completely.

When the clay piece has cooled completely, glue on a pin back, a button-cover finding, or an earring post. I sometimes brush a little metallic powder (see Resources on p. 91) on the shard to add a touch of iridescence to the piece. Brush the front with a matte lacquer, then glue any jewels or beads in place, keeping holes in the beads horizontal so they're out of sight.

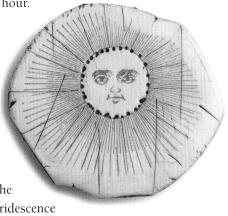

Gorgeous Beaded Buttons:
Make Just One or a Set

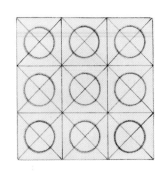

Bead irresistible little jewels, disguised as buttons, to complete a special garment or to give as gifts.

Whether it's a single, dramatic button or a distinctive set for your next project—or a gift for a sewing friend— try making beaded buttons. It's fun, inexpensive, and easier than it looks. These buttons can vary in size and be as simple or elaborate as you want. You can incorporate a detailed pattern or an image from a charted design. And though these buttons look delicate, they're quite sturdy and can even be handwashed if you use the recommended supplies.

GATHER THE BASICS

A little goes a long way for these buttons, so leftovers from other projects may suffice. In addition to a beading needle and good-quality beading thread (see Resources on p. 91), you'll need small quantities of seed beads (size 12 or smaller); bugles and/or accent beads; and if you want to bead a charted design, small, cylindrical Japanese Delica Beads™.

For backing fabric on which to bead, use either rubberized flannel sheeting or craft felt stabilized with fusible interfacing; a 9-in. by 12-in. piece of backing is sufficient for most button sets. You'll also need a fine-point permanent pen, silk or polyester buttonhole twist thread for the shank, a tapestry needle, and small amounts of fusible web and Ultrasuede™ or Ultrasuede Light in a coordinating color for the backing.

PREPARE THE FABRIC, AND THEN BEAD

If you're beading on felt, first fuse the interfacing to the felt. Fuse the fusible web to the Ultrasuede, and set aside.

To make a set of buttons that all match, work them side by side on a grid marked on the backing with a permanent pen, as shown in the drawing at left. And always make an extra button in case one gets lost or damaged.

Grid Marked for Round Button Set

For a matched button set, mark grid on backing, and then draw in button shapes. Area marked for beading is ⅛ in. to ¼ in. smaller than finished button because final picot edge will take up this space.

Buttons can be round, triangular, oval, or square in any size from ½ in. to 1½ in. Patterns and charted images work best on a larger button. Working a beaded picot edge will add from ⅛ in. to ¼ in. to the final size.

Begin beading at the button's center. One of the quickest buttons to bead is a grid of bugle bead squares sewn in alternating directions and separated by rows of seed beads. To secure bugles and larger accent beads, use a triple backstitch, passing the needle through each bead three times.

Another simple, distinctive button starts with a seed or accent bead at the center and has concentric circles of seed beads sewn around it. For buttons like those shown here, attach the beads with the two-bead overlay stitch as shown above right. When beading a concentric row, use the same color bead throughout or alternate colors in close or contrasting tones. After finishing a concentric row, run the needle and thread back through the entire row, a few beads at a time, then pull the thread to tighten and neaten the circle. Backstitch through the felt to secure before beginning the next one.

You can draw a motif like that on the flower button at right directly on the felt, then bead it like a paint-by-numbers kit. Or draw a more elaborate design on graph paper, and bead one horizontal row at a time.

QUICK STEPS TO THE FINISH

After you finish beading, cut the Ultrasuede to match the shape of the beaded fabric. Fuse it to the beaded fabric's wrong side, placing the beading face down on a towel and using a press cloth.

When the layers have cooled, cut out each button, trimming the margin flush with the outermost beaded row. Bead the picot

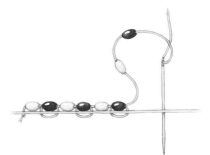

Two-Bead Overlay Stitch

Bring threaded needle to RS, pick up two beads, and insert needle two bead lengths away. Backstitch between beads and through last bead. Pick up two more beads and repeat.

edge as shown in the drawing below from the right side, stitching through all layers to produce a clean edge. To finish, sew on a thread shank using a buttonhole twist. Or glue on a purchased button or pin back using a jewelry glue like E6000. ●

Match all the buttons in a set by working them on a grid.

Beaded Picot Edge

Bring threaded needle to edge of button. Pick up one bead, take stitch at edge through all layers, and insert needle through bead. Now add two beads, take stitch short distance away, and insert needle through last bead. Repeat, adding two beads each time, around circumference of button.

Cliché but true: The right embellishment can truly turn an ordinary item into something extraordinary. Add a bit of ribbon to a pillow or an embroidered detail to a garment to give each a distinctive look. Don't pine for dévoré—that beautiful cut velvet that can be so pricey—it's easy to create  your own for a fraction of the cost. Can't draw but love hand-painted fabric? Use those ubiquitous ink stamps. And don't just stamp designs on your fabric—enhance your stamped patterns with fabric pens and embroidery details for remarkable results. ●

part 2

Embellishments

Stamped Fabric Is Only the Beginning

*i*f, like me, you're captivated by all the wonderful rubber stamp designs available today, you'll be glad to know how easy it is to get a really terrific image on fabric. Not only is fabric stamping instantly gratifying and full of possiblities for creative expression, but I've also discovered that you can enhance the stamped image even further. I like to draw over the image with fabric pens to increase its depth and detail. Then I embroider some of the design with tiny French knots and other embroidery stitches. Once you've learned how to detail your stamped images, you can bring them to life on all kinds of fabric accessories, from fabric-covered boxes, ribbons, and tea-towels, to evening bags, scarves, trim, pillows, bed linens, and garments.

Stamp images on a fabric-covered box and coordinating ribbon for a personalized gift. And stamp a fabric gift to make a complete package. A few embroidery stitches sweeten the designs on these handmade tea towels.

GETTING STARTED

You'll need a few supplies from a craft-supply store or by mail order. First, of course, are stamps, ink pads, and fabric. I like the images available from Personal Stamp Exchange (see Resources on p. 91), but shop for the ones that intrigue you most. When choosing an ink-pad color, remember that for this method, a light color will allow the added detailing to have more impact.

The best fabrics for showing off the stamped image are tightly woven plain-weaves, such as cotton batiste, broadcloth, or organdy. Finely woven linen is also good for stamping and, surprisingly, so is unprinted flannel. If you like silk, try habutai (also known as China silk), crepe de Chine, dupioni, taffeta, broadcloth, or satin. Be sure to select a fabric that's light to medium in

All you need to get started stamping is fabric, stamps, ink pads, a marker, and a pen. Choose coordinating colors, and experiment to find the best fabric for stamping.

tone, so the stamped image won't be obscured. I like to use related or closely matched colors of inks on a lighter fabric in the same color for a tone-on-tone effect.

For detailing the stamped image, I use a dual-tip permanent marker, such as Fabrico™, and a fine-point permanent-ink gel pen, like Gelly Roll™. Gelly Roll pens come in many colors, some of which are metallic.

Finally, to add a little embroidery to the design, you'll need some cotton embroidery floss and a hand-sewing needle. I like to use standard embroidery needles in sizes ranging from 3 to 9.

READY, SET, STAMP

To ensure a crisp image, place flat cardboard (not corrugated) or several sheets of paper on a worktable. Position the fabric, right side up, on this surface. Tap or press the ink pad lightly onto the stamp (not the other way around, as you might be tempted to do), making sure all the design elements have a coat of ink. Be sure not to press the pad too hard onto the stamp, or you'll overcoat the stamp and blur the image. Next press the stamp onto a test swatch of fabric, holding it in place for 3 to 20 seconds, without rocking it: the more complex a stamp design, the longer the pressing time. To complete the process, lift the stamp straight up from the fabric. When you're finished stamping, be sure to clean your rubber stamp with stamp cleaner or baby wipes. If you plan to wash the fabric, heat-set the images with an iron, using a press cloth.

DETAILING THE IMAGE

To detail and deepen the stamped image, darken the broader lines in the image with the dual-tip marker and a light touch. Use the brush end of the marker on lines that are $\frac{1}{32}$ in. wide or more. Use the fine-tip end of

the marker for smaller lines; this end will make a darker line than the brush end. The marker works fine on cottons and linens, but on some silks, the ink will bleed instantly, even with a light touch. Always test on a scrap first, and if the marker bleeds, skip this step.

Use the permanent-ink gel pen to draw over design lines to define the detail in the image. Refer to the rubber stamp when detailing—some of its finer lines may appear faint on the fabric, and you might miss them.

EMBROIDER THE DESIGN

I like to add a few hand-embroidered stitches to the final images, which not only sets my stamped fabric apart from the others but also adds a subtle textural effect to the detailing. You need only basic embroidery stitches, such as the outline stitch, French knot, lazy daisy, and straight stitch. I've used two strands of embroidery floss to create a delicate touch on the towels shown above, but silk ribbon embroidery on a larger stamped image would also be quite pretty.

Let your imagination play with the process of stamping and detailing. It's lots of fun and provides wonderful handmade holiday gifts. And while you're at it, why not stamp paper gift wrap and coordinating ribbon too? ●

To create a subtle three-dimensional stamped image, start with an ink color lighter than you'd ordinarily want. After heat-setting the stamped image with an iron, emphasize the larger design lines with a dual-tip marker and the smaller lines with a gel pen. To finish, embroider over some of the lines on the stamped image.

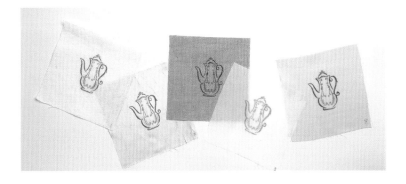

Your Very Own Dévoré Velvet

Seeing the luscious dévoré velvets in designer fashion collections started my fingers itching and gave me the urge to try creating some unique velvet fabrics of my own. The word dévoré (French for "devoured") aptly describes the burn-out process that produces this fabric: A chemical solution eats away the velvet's rayon pile in areas where it's applied, leaving the silk backing intact and creating beautiful patterns. Cut velvets make stellar scarves or garment details like lapels and pockets.

Starting with one of these fluid rayon/silk velvets (usually 82 percent rayon/18 percent silk), I experimented with a product called Fiber Etch® Fabric Remover to remove parts of the pile (see Resources on p. 91 for both velvets and Fiber Etch). This thick gel is convenient and easy to work with, but if you need a large quantity, you can also concoct your own mixture, which must be used within two days. Request the recipe from Silkpaint (see Resources). They also sell P4 Thickener, one of the main ingredients; you can buy the other ingredients at a chemical-supply house.

THE BURN-OUT PROCESS

In a nutshell, the burn-out process involves applying a thin layer of gel to the wrong side of the fabric, allowing it to dry naturally or with a hair dryer (who can wait?), then using heat to produce the chemical reaction, washing to remove the pile and dried gel, and finally machine-drying the fabric.

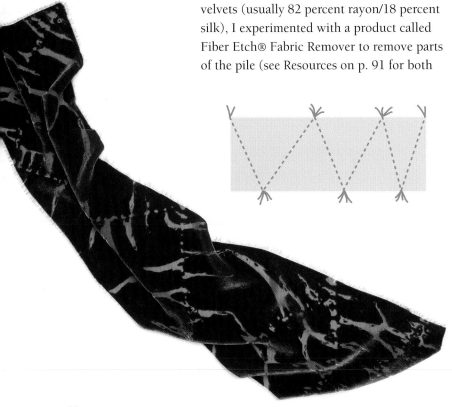

To create naturalistic, abstract patterns, adapt shibori dyeing techniques. This scarf was created by machine-stitching across the fabric in the zigzag pattern shown. The fabric was gathered along the stitching lines, and burn-out gel was applied to the tops of the gathers and folds, producing a striated effect.

FIRST DREAM UP A DESIGN

Now for the fun part. You can create designs with the gel in a variety of ways. I suggest you start by doodling with the gel on samples to see what effects you like and which technique removes the pile cleanly.

Freehand and stencils

Freehand squiggles applied straight from the bottle result in skinny lines that don't show up, but if you spread the bead of gel gently with a clean paintbrush, pressing it into the fabric, the line will have more impact (see the left end of the fabric at top right).

Stencils and stickers create negative and positive design areas in the pile, respectively. Try an office-supply store for press-on labels in a range of sizes and shapes. For the fabric shown at bottom right, I combined labels with stick-on numerals, photo-mounting corners, hole reinforcements, and cut-up decorative seals. I first placed the stickers in a pleasing design, then squirted gel in the open spaces and used a paintbrush to press it in and create a thin, even layer in areas I wanted to excise.

Shibori

You can get great, organic-looking design effects by using techniques borrowed from shibori dyeing. Try wrapping a piece of velvet around a wine bottle (for a larger piece of fabric, use a length of PVC pipe), gathering and tying one end of the fabric to the top of the bottle with polyester thread, and tightly wrapping the fabric to the other end, securing it with tape. Arrange the fabric so there are many small folds, and scrunch it together so the folds are tight. Now apply the gel to the tops of all the folds, again using a paintbrush to evenly distribute it. Leave the fabric on the bottle while the gel dries.

Freehand brushing, stickers, and stencils yield a variety of geometric patterns limited only by your imagination. Shown below is a design of hieroglyphics made with shapes cut from stick-on labels, and above is a sampler of ideas, including spiral doodles applied right from the Fiber-Etch bottle, then brushed, and a Greek key design made with stick-on strips.

Quick Tip

Directions always tell you to test thoroughly, but for this technique it's really important. You can end up with uneven results if you don't experiment first.

A second shibori method, shown on the fabric on p. 24, involves stitching on the fabric first. With the machine's longest (6 mm) straight stitches, sew a large zigzag design across the fabric, as shown in the diagram on p. 24, leaving long thread tails at the beginning and end of each "zig." Then tie off one end of each "zig," pull up the thread to gather the fabric, and tie off the other end. Repeat for all the stitching. Lay the fabric flat, apply gel to the brush, and paint along the stitching lines and on top of the fabric's gathers and folds.

Silk-screening

The manufacturer also suggests a simple silk-screen method, which I haven't tried yet but which sounds interesting: Stretch a piece of polyester organza or other evenly woven sheer in an embroidery hoop, cut a design in contact paper, and press it on top of the hooped fabric. Lay the hoop on the velvet, placing it where you want the design to appear. Smooth the gel across the hooped design with a credit-card "squeegee," pressing the gel into the velvet.

Quick Tip

Although burn-out gel is not a toxic blend of chemicals, it makes sense to protect your skin and surfaces from possible damage. So wear gloves when handling, and cover work areas with a plastic sheet or newspapers. Since pile dust can be irritating when inhaled, wear a mask if you're sensitive. And if gel gets on clothing or skin, wash it off with soap and water.

FINISHING YOUR FABRIC

Allow your gel to dry naturally, or dry it with a hair dryer. Now you are ready for the heat stage, which will produce the chemical reaction. You have two choices: Instructions for Fiber Etch suggest using a clothes dryer on velvet to avoid crushing the pile, but out of impatience I reverted to the ironing technique described for other fabrics. (I figured that since the fabric still needed to be washed, then dried in the dryer, the final drying would fluff up any crushed pile.) In fact, a dry iron at a silk/wool setting and a thin press cloth placed on the wrong side of the fabric work well to activate the gel.

After ironing, scratch the pile with a fingernail to see if it's ready to fall out. The flat side of a credit card or flat plastic pot scraper is perfect for gently scraping away the pile. While it's true that rinsing removes the burned-out pile, it also removes the dried gel, so be sure your design has come out cleanly before rinsing. If it hasn't, iron a little more with the press cloth in place, then scrape again. Be careful not to let the iron get too hot or to hold it too long in one place. Otherwise, the dried gel may burn, especially in spots where it has been thickly applied, and this, in turn, can cause holes in the silk backing.

Well, I'm hooked! And I can't wait to get my hands on some iridescent velvet, which has the backing and pile woven in two different colors. Just imagine the gorgeous effects you could get by burning away part of the pile on a navy/burgundy velvet! ●

1

Dimensional Embroidery

*i*f you enjoy doing both hand- and machine-embroidery, why not combine the two approaches to get the dimensional effect of hand embroidery and the convenience and speed of working on a sewing machine. In the samples on this and the following two pages, the foliage of the three-dimensional bouquets is machine-embroidered and the flowers are worked with various traditional hand-embroidery techniques.

START WITH THE BACKGROUND FOLIAGE

The greenery in these bouquets was created on a sewing machine equipped to use computer memory cards containing preprogrammed designs with an attachable embroidery hoop. You can produce similar results using decorative stitches on a programmable sewing machine or in the old-fashioned way, with free-motion machine embroidery and satin stitching.

For each bouquet, I embroidered the foliage first, then added the flowers by hand. Much of the success of a dimensional-embroidery piece depends on creating a background that gives the illusion of depth. Here's how to achieve dimensionality in your machine-embroidered foliage.

Add dimension with your color choices

Unless you're using preprogrammed machine-embroidery cards, which tell you what colors to use, the first step—after deciding on a design for the foliage—is to select thread colors. Three different shades of green are all you really need to create depth in machine-embroidered foliage. Begin by selecting the main green you want for most of the foliage in the design. Then choose the greens for the background and foreground, keeping in mind two guidelines that artists use to create dimension in a design: Bright colors appear close up, while dull colors look far away; and warm tones (reds and yellows) look near, while cool tones (blues) recede into the distance.

With these principles in mind, select a green for the background that's duller and cooler (bluer) than the main green. And, to create the foreground, choose a green that's darker, brighter, and warmer (with more yellow in it) than the main green you're using.

Add more colors

If you want to add other shades of green to the first

Hand-embroidered flowers can be added in minutes to a background of machine-embroidered foliage. The flowers in samples 1, 2, 4, 7, 8, and 9 were embroidered with various sizes of silk ribbon. Sample 3 combines silk-ribbon embroidery with Russian needle-punch in the flowers' centers. Samples 5 and 6 feature Russian needle-punch flowers. The flowers in samples 10 and 11 were made with Brazilian embroidery.

2

3

4

three, select colors in accordance with a third guideline for adding dimension to your design: A pair of bright, contrasting colors (one light and one dark) placed side by side will appear close up, while a pair of low-contrast colors that are similar in value (both light or both dark) will look far away.

Overlap colors

Begin by stitching a quarter of the foliage using your background color. Next, stitch a little more than half the foliage in your main color. (Most of these leaves should overlap the background foliage.) Finally, use your brightest color to stitch the remaining leaves, which will overlap some of the first two layers to create the foreground.

ADD MORE DIMENSION WITH HAND-WORKED FLOWERS

Once the foliage has been machine-stitched, you can add bright, colorful flowers worked by hand in minutes. I made the flowers shown here using three techniques: silk-ribbon embroidery, Russian needlepunch work, and Brazilian embroidery. If you're unfamiliar with one or more of these beautiful techniques, there are many how-to books available.

You can use the same color guidelines outlined above for producing a three-dimensional effect with the flowers, or you can use slight variations of shade and tone within the flowers. Silk embroidery ribbon is available in a rainbow of colors and in 2-mm, 4-mm, and 7-mm widths. You can either mix different-colored ribbons as

5

6

7

shown in sample 4 to add visual interest or dye the ribbon to get the subtle color variations for a particular design. Since a punch-needle will carry two different threads at once, you can combine two shades or types of thread for this technique. For example, in sample 5, a glittery metallic thread mixed with a soft embroidery floss gives a dewy appearance.

Samples 10 and 11 show Brazilian embroidery, which traditionally uses rayon thread and produces stitches with a characteristic stiffness. You can also try mixing variegated threads to achieve different results, and use a bouclé for even more texture. And by mixing different thread weights in a single design, you can produce variations in flower sizes.

CREATIVITY COUNTS

Whether you're adding a splash of color to a cuff or collar or embellishing a large surface, once you've begun to play with the idea of blending hand and machine embroidery, the possibilities are endless. Try machine-stitching some background flowers along with the foliage or hand-stitching some of the foreground leaves along with the flowers. When you combine the beauty of traditional needlework with the convenience of computerized technology, you'll discover that the sky's the limit. ●

8

9

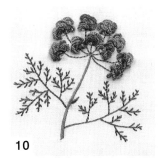

10

11

Take the Ribbon Road

"road-mapping"—stitching silk ribbon or flat braid to fabric to resemble an abstract road map—is a fun departure from the usual embellished decorating project. The ribbon stitchery can be subtle or lively, adding just the right look to your interior. Silk ribbon is so easy to work with and comes in such delectable shades—you can also dye your own—that it makes perfect road-map material.

I prefer silk ribbon because it's pliable, which makes it easy to shape. It comes in a variety of sizes, from 4 mm to 50 mm (I like 4 mm, 7 mm, and sometimes 13 mm). It is available in a plain weave, for muted luster, as well as in a shiny satin weave. Bias-cut silk ribbon, mostly available in lovely hand-dyed combinations, adds a pleasing texture to a map if the edges are frayed.

There are also other natural-fiber ribbons suitable for road-mapping; I like rayon or rayon-blend ribbons, which are sometimes loosely woven or have picot edges. Fancy braids, if lightweight, soft, and narrow, are wonderful for road-mapping on upholstery fabric, as on the pillow shown below. And some machine-embroidery threads are wide enough to create the road-map texture. Even though there are plenty of ribbons and braids to choose from, ordinary silk ribbon on a sheer fabric, as on the curtain shown on the facing page, makes a luxurious design—and a good first project.

Woven braid is a good choice for "mapping" an upholstered pillow. It's flat, pliable and has pizazz that would overwhelm a delicate project. On the road-mapped scarf below, silk ribbon woven on the bias frays attractively without unraveling.

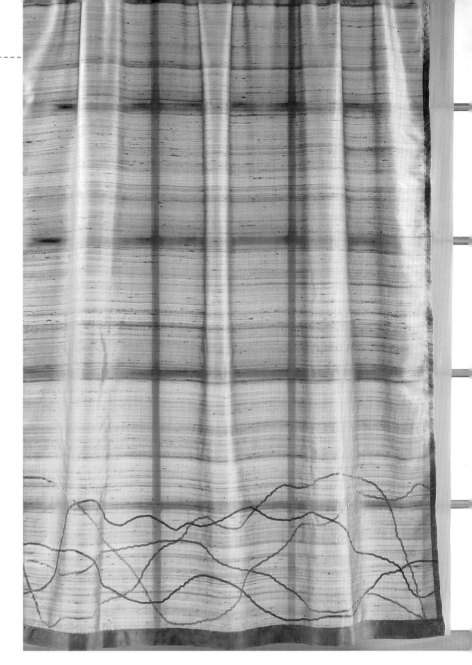

Silk ribbon road-mapped on a delicate curtain enhances a window and blends naturally with the room's colors. Silk ribbon is subtly lustrous and handles wonderfully.

HIT THE ROAD

After gathering, say, three to five ribbons, lay them haphazardly on the fabric. Do the ribbon and fabric colors harmonize? Try adding to or subtracting from the collection.

Pin the ribbons in place on the fabric, bending them to resemble the twists and turns of a road map. Use standard sewing threads matching the fabric to hand-tack the ribbon into place, alternating edges with each stitch (see the bottom photo at right). It's unnecessary for the ribbon to lie flat; the next step takes care of that.

The silk-ribbon stitching is now ready to become a road map. Turn the fabric over, and steam-press on the wrong side. This step causes the ribbon to "settle" into the design.

Without the distraction of a recognizable design in abstract ribbon maps, the qualities of the materials take center stage. And as your eye wanders along the ribbon road, your mind can wander, too. ●

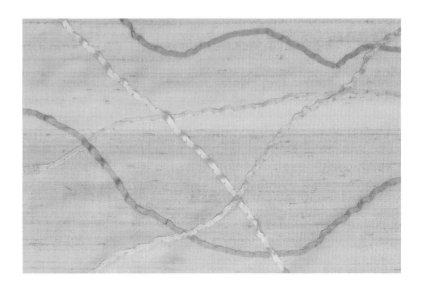

Alternating stitches on each edge of the ribbon makes road-mapping easy. No fancy embroidery stitches or thread needed—just match the color.

Accessories can transform the look of an outfit in an instant. And few things dress up an outfit the way a scarf can, especially if you begin with a special fabric or incorporate embellishments like beads—materials you might consider too costly to use for a garment. Here you'll find several variations  on the scarf theme. In addition, we share clever ideas for creating belts and bags. And who doesn't wish for a quick-to-sew garment that really delivers on its promise? We present a simple summer skirt and a shrug—both offer lots of versatility and can be made in a snap. ●

part 3

Wearables

Call 'em Irresistible— Beads and Tulle

Soft, fine tulle has a way of cradling beads without dimming their light. To us, the effect resembles light filtering through trees. Who can resist this elusive combination, whether to wear for an opulent evening out, or to trim a good sweater or wool suit?

The scarf and shawl on these pages show two different ways to combine these delicious materials. Our pieces aren't made with exact patterns for the beads. The scarf blends seed beads with two sizes of faceted crystals in a random, meandering pattern on both sides, so there's no right or wrong side. The shawl, which we call "Rain," is a more orderly design, covered with equal-size dangles that combine seed beads and round, clear crystals, with each unit anchored by a single clear sequin. What makes the shawl interesting is the random, organic placement of the dangles—denser on the ends and scattered toward the center. When the shawl is worn, gravity causes all the dangles to hang in the same direction, which gives the piece its name.

BEADS, BEADS, AND TULLE

You can use the soft tulle available in fabric stores, although some of our favorite colors are custom dyed. You'll find seed beads and crystal beads at many bead stores, or by mail from the Bead Warehouse (see Resources on p. 91).

For our scarf, we chose tulle in a soft blond color with pale gray beads, but it would also be beautiful in gray or taupe tulle with clear beads. You'll need an unhemmed piece of tulle 15 in. by 40 in. for the scarf and about 1,200 size 11 or 12 seed beads; around 275 faceted 4-mm Austrian crystals; and 13 round faceted 10-mm crystals, which give the piece its wonderful weight and drape. For our huge pure-white shawl, we start with 3 yd. of 54-in.-wide unhemmed tulle and add more than

Sew a Meandering Beaded Scarf

An Easy Dangle
With knotted length of thread, sew into seed bead, large crystal bead, and second seed bead. Bring needle back through large crystal and first seed bead and tighten, then add more beads to complete dangle. Anchor at edge of tulle with backstitches.

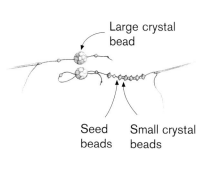

Large crystal bead

Seed beads

Small crystal beads

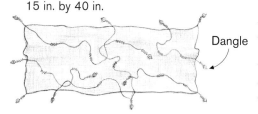

15 in. by 40 in.

Dangle

Start with dangle, then bead edge of tulle, and end with second dangle. When edges are complete, add curving lines of beads to interior.

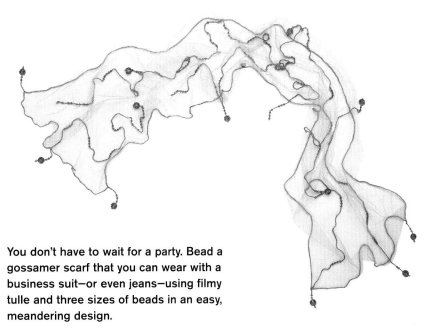

1,000 dangles. For 1,000 dangles, you'll need around 12,000 size 11 or 12 clear seed beads; 1,000 clear sequins; and 1,000 smooth round 4-mm crystals.

We prefer to sew the beads with size 24 glazed cotton thread, which is sold on large spools at tailoring and dressmaker-supply stores like Oregon Tailor Supply (see Resources on p. 91).

While many beaders choose nylon thread for strength, we find that the knots tied in nylon aren't secure enough for this type of beading. As a substitute, you can try a cotton-wrapped polyester thread. Experiment to find a needle that you like, with an eye large enough to thread but small enough to pass through the tiny seed beads. We prefer to use a size 10 beading needle.

IT BEGINS WITH A "DANGLE"

The basic design unit for the scarf and shawl is a beaded dangle. In the drawing at on the facing page, you can see just how easy this is to make.

Bead the meandering scarf

In the same drawing, you'll see that the scarf is made with a continuous line of beads along each edge and a few meandering bead lines in the center, each starting and ending with a beaded dangle. For the first row, begin with a length of thread twice that of the scarf, or 80 in.; thread the needle and

You don't have to wait for a party. Bead a gossamer scarf that you can wear with a business suit—or even jeans—using filmy tulle and three sizes of beads in an easy, meandering design.

A "Rain" shawl hovers around the shoulders like a cloud. It's made with easy-to-sew crystal and seed beads on tulle.

Design for Rain Shawl

Sew dangle as shown below, and anchor to tulle. Place dangles more densely at ends of shawl, gradually thinning toward center.

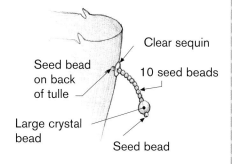

Clear sequin

Seed bead on back of tulle

10 seed beads

Large crystal bead

Seed bead

A Raindrop Dangle

Start as for basic dangle (see drawing on p. 34), add sequin, pass needle to other side of tulle, and add seed bead. Return to front through sequin, and knot thread.

knot one end. Spear a seed bead, a large crystal bead, and a second seed bead, then pass the needle back through the large crystal and the first seed bead; the crystal will hide the knot. Continue by alternating a small crystal bead with a seed bead until you've reached the desired length of the dangle (about six small crystal beads). To secure the dangle, sew a couple of backstitches into a corner of the tulle.

Now continue sewing along the long edge of the scarf, adding six seed beads on one side of the tulle, passing the needle to the other side, and picking up six seed beads on this side. Repeat this pattern to the opposite end of the scarf, secure the thread with a couple of backstitches, and sew the second dangle, working in reverse order to the first

dangle. End by passing the needle back through the large crystal and to the top of the dangle; knot the thread, insert the needle through the top seed bead, and knot the thread again.

Continue around the scarf in this manner. After you finish the edges, sew some meandering rows on the interior of the scarf. On these, we often toss in a group of small crystals or a single dangle, so the design isn't too predictable. Just plan the beading as you go along, and sew an arrangement that pleases you.

Create beaded rain

Each dangle on the shawl is constructed in the same way as the initial one on the scarf, except with different beads. Start with a seed bead; a smooth clear crystal bead; and another seed bead. Then pass the needle back through the crystal and first seed bead and add nine more seed beads and a clear sequin. Secure the dangle to the tulle with a couple of stitches, then pass the needle to the other side, add a seed bead, and go back through the sequin to knot off; cut the thread.

Basically, you can add as many dangles as you can stand to sew! At the ends of the shawl, we scatter them a few inches apart, increasing the distance between dangles as we approach the center of the shawl.

NOT JUST FOR SCARVES

Once you've made a scarf or shawl, you can easily apply the same methods to, say, a sheer tulle T-shirt with a meandering beaded design, which you can wear over a sleek body suit. Or try a beaded sleeve—or a pocket or collar—on a plain organza or silk crepe blouse. And when you wear your creation, you'll feel like you're standing in dappled sunlight. ●

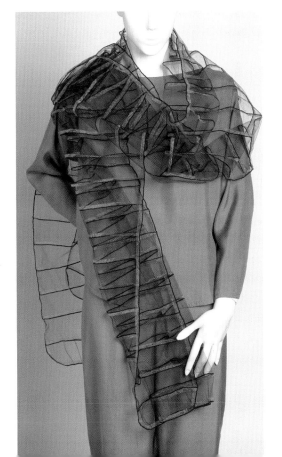

Gossamer Ribbon-Work Scarves

imagine an airy scarf made from nothing but yards and yards of sheer ribbon that drapes around your shoulders like a cloud. We call this scarf Ombre because it creates a play of light and shadow (see the photo below right). It's made entirely from knotted lengths of ribbon, interlinked to form a fabric. Or the same sheer ribbon can be combined with tulle to create a delicately striped shawl (below left), which we call Mirage. Each style is simple to make, and the first requires absolutely no sewing! We'll explain the easy step-by-step directions so you can

try these delicious accessories for yourself or for holiday gifts.

A SIMPLE TOOL KIT

The knotted scarf requires nothing more than ribbon, scissors, and a flat place to work. We usually cut the ends of the ribbon at a slight angle to reduce raveling, even though this ribbon doesn't fray easily. A small fringed end would look okay, too.

To assemble the tulle-and-ribbon shawl, we use a commercial pearl-edge overlock machine, but you can get a similar effect with a three-thread rolled hem on a home serger. Experiment on samples, and adjust your serger to produce a dense, narrow stitch.

Layered sheers create a play of light and shadow. For the striped shawl at far left, use a serger to join strips of tulle to sheer ribbon. If you can tie a square knot, you can make the easy, knotted-ribbon scarf at left which moves with every breeze.

Knot an Ombre Ribbon Scarf

Work on a large flat surface, so you can spread out the loops and see where you're going. Cut 140 strips of ribbon, each 13 in. long.

FIRST ROW: Tie ends of one strip in square knot to form circle, leaving 1½ -in.-long ends. Link second strip through first and tie same way, creating two linked circles. Repeat until you have nine linked circles of ribbon, spread out in a straight line.

SECOND ROW: Place a strip of ribbon through first two circles of first row and tie. Repeat with second and subsequent circles to end of row, but do not link to other circles of second row. Tie a circle through eighth circle of row; do not attach to first row.

THIRD ROW: Beginning at end of second row, place strip through eighth and ninth circles creating first circle of third row. Continue as for second row, leaving ninth link of third row detached from first link of second row.

Third row

Second row

First row

1 2 3 4 5 6 7 8 9

Repeat for 18 rows.

THE RIBBON MAKES THE DIFFERENCE

The ½-in.-wide gauzy, nylon-organdy ribbon that works so well for this scarf and shawl is, fortunately, relatively inexpensive, and you'll need quite a lot of it. For the knotted scarf, you'll need 51 yd. to make a 30-in. square (the knotted fabric easily collapses to become a 12-in. by 50-in. rectangle; it's worn like a boa). The large 27-in. by 108-in. striped shawl requires 2 yd. of 54-in.-wide tulle and 42 yd. of ribbon, but it's easy to adapt the style to smaller sizes. You will find

several brands of nylon organdy ribbon on the market, imported from France or Japan.

The unique variegated ribbon we use makes our scarves special. It shades gently from one color to the next, so the colors blend subtly within the scarf. We've used two subtle color combinations: slate, bronze, and mahogany and light copper, gray-blue, and olive. You'll be able to find similar ribbons to create an ombre effect (see Resources on p. 91).

You can also make a beautiful single-color scarf or buy smaller amounts of two or three plain colors to mix randomly for your own

Diagram for Sheer Mirage Shawl

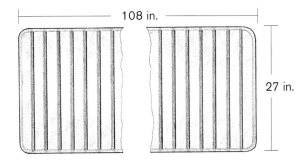

|← 108 in. →|

27 in.

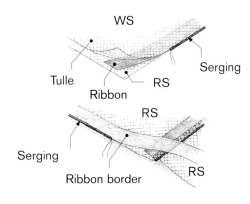

WS

Tulle

Ribbon

RS

Serging

Serging

Ribbon border

RS

RS

color combination. Some organdy ribbons come in a ⅜-in. width, instead of ½ in.; either width works fine for both the scarf and shawl.

EASY CONSTRUCTION STEPS

The knotted scarf is a breeze to make. Just follow the easy steps shown on the facing page to cut the ribbon, then tie the loops in order. For the striped shawl, first cut the tulle into 46 3-in. by 27-in. strips (fewer for a shorter shawl and narrower for a scarf), and cut 45 pieces of ribbon, each 27 in. long. Finally, cut one 7½-yd. length of ribbon, which you'll use to finish the shawl's edges.

Beginning and ending with a tulle strip, serge the tulle and ribbon strips together in alternating sequence, allowing the serger blades to trim off about ⅛ in. of the ribbon.

When all the strips have been joined to create one fabric, serge the 7½-yd. piece of ribbon around the outside edges, slightly rounding the corners. This final step frames the entire shawl. ●

Stitch an Easy Bra-Slip

Why wear two garments when a single one will do the job nicely? A bra-slip or bra-camisole combines two lingerie layers into one easy-to-wear piece, neatly eliminating a set of slippery straps that don't align with your bra straps, and creating a smooth line under clothing. And you'll find it quick and easy to sew if you start with a purchased bra and sew the slip to complement it.

START WITH A BRA YOU LIKE

First, select a well-fitting bra with a back opening. An underwire bra is fine, as long as the wire lies above the lower band (so you can zigzag along the edge without hitting the wire). If you'd like to add lace to the bottom of the slip or camisole, as I did on the slip at left, you'll probably want to choose a white, beige, or black bra, since you'll find a wider lace selection in these colors. Or you can make a turned-and-stitched hem at the lower edge, finished with straight, twin-needle, or decorative stitching.

I prefer to eliminate the back opening of the bra so the slip will fit smoothly at the back, but you may need an opening, depending on your shape and size and the bra style you select. Try the bra on to see whether the band has enough elasticity to slide on and off without opening the back. Removing the hooks and eyes and joining the ends will make the band circumference 1 in. smaller than the tightest hook closing, so be sure to select the size accordingly.

If you decide to retain the bra's back opening, you'll need an opening in the slip as well. It can be a simple 4-in.-long slit with a bias binding, a narrow, stitched-down facing, or a narrow lace edge finish.

CHOOSE A FABRIC

Select a slip fabric that complements the bra. Silk or polyester crepe de Chine, charmeuse, and jacquards are luxurious options, and nylon tricot is always a practical choice. If you choose silk, prewash it, testing a swatch first to be sure that you like any changes in the color and texture of the fabric.

MAKE A SIMPLE SLIP PATTERN

Draw an easy pattern for the slip on paper. If you're using a woven fabric, cut the slip on the bias for a smooth drape and fit. Cut knits like tricot with the lengthwise grain along the center front and back.

To calculate the pattern length, measure from the lower edge of the bra to the desired length. Add 2 in. or more for the upper seam allowance and hem.

SUPER-EASY CONSTRUCTION

Open the pattern and cut one front and one back panel, marking the top centers with tiny snips. Sew the side seams using French seams, an overlock stitch, or a serger. If you want a back opening for the slip, complete it now.

To eliminate the bra's back opening, cut off the hooks and eyes, overlap the band ends about ⅜ in., and anchor the ends with two rows of zigzagging. Try on the bra and mark the location for the side seams on the bra band, then remove it and divide the front and back sections in half to mark the center front and back. Don't be surprised if the front and back aren't equal—bras are often more elastic at the back.

Pin the bra to the slip, overlapping the cut edge about 1 in. Match side marks and centers and pin, distributing the ease evenly. Machine-baste, stretching the band just enough to fit the slip. If the front band of the bra has a contour edge, baste the back section only. Try on the slip and adjust the front overlap for a smooth fit. Run a chalk pencil or marker along the lower edge of the bra to mark the seamline, then baste to check the fit. Starting at the center back, sew along the lower edge of the bra band, using a zigzag stitch 2-mm wide and long. Stitch again ¼ in. away, or press the seam toward the slip and stitch again over the first zigzag; either way, trim close to the stitching.

Add lace at the lower edge, or turn the hem under twice and sew. And that's it! In the time it takes to shop for lingerie, you've made yourself a custom-fitted bra-slip. ●

French-seam basics
French seam encloses raw edges, perfect for slip's side seams. With WSs together, stitch seam at half seam-allowance width, then press, trim allowance to ⅛ in., fold RSs together, and stitch again ¼ in. from fold.

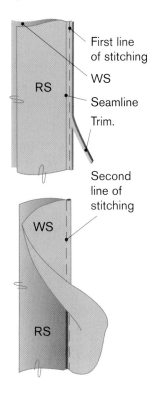

First line of stitching

WS

Seamline

Trim.

RS

WS

Second line of stitching

RS

Draw a Simple Slip Pattern

To make full pattern (easier for cutting on bias), fold paper in half; foldline becomes center front and back. Draw line for top edge as shown. Measure rib cage and fullest hip, add 2 in. or more of ease, and divide each by 4; measure length from edge of bra to hip and mark points on pattern. Mark slip length and draw line for lower edge.

Connect rib cage and hip dots as shown, continuing A-shape to hem. Add seam allowance by drawing parallel line ⅝ in. away. Mark lengthwise grain (on bias for wovens, along fold for knits).

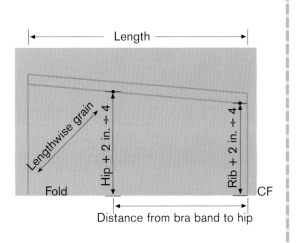

Length

Lengthwise grain

Hip + 2 in. ÷ 4

Rib + 2 in. ÷ 4

Fold

CF

Distance from bra band to hip

Seashells to Wear

*t*he treasures you bring back from those warm vacation walks on the beach don't have to collect dust on a windowsill. Using a sewn fabric bezel (or frame), you can mount a large seashell, flat rock, or other find to wear on a belt or bag, or even a vest. It's easy to draw around the natural shape to adapt the bezel pattern to fit it. Or, for a smaller treasure, you can fashion a thread bezel from several rounds of buttonhole stitches.

WHICH TREASURES WORK BEST?

Choose a shell that's fairly flat on the back, so it will lie smoothly on the surface. If it has a domed shape on top, like the shell on the belt shown above, you'll probably want to drill four to six tiny holes near the edge (I use a Dremel™ drill with a number 80 bit) and hand-sew the shell to the surface for security. On a flatter shape, the bezel alone may be enough to securely hold the shell in place.

A SEWN FABRIC BEZEL

After drawing around the shell on plain paper, draw lines inside and outside the shape, as shown in the drawing on the facing page, to create the bezel width and seam allowances. If you make a belt of nonraveling Ultrasuede, like the one shown above, you really don't have to finish the edges of the bezel. I decided to sew a finished seam at the inner edge but not the outer one, so I included an inner seam allowance on my drawing.

Trace your drawing to make a pattern and cut it out of two layers of Ultrasuede, with right sides together. Sew the bezel's inner edge with the paper pattern pinned on top, using short machine stitches. Clip the seam allowance every ⅛ in., turn the layers to be wrong sides together, and press, then sew

---

Design **idea**

A Neat Hidden Closure

*m*y belt has an adjustable hook-and-loop-tape closure hidden at the belt's back. To add a similar closure to your belt pattern (this one is KWIK SEW® 2119), add 3 in. to the right end of the belt. Stitch a narrow tube of fabric to serve as a belt loop (4 in. long for my 1½-in.-wide belt), then butt the ends and hand-sew to join securely.

To complete the closure, slide the loop onto the finished left end of the belt, fold the end under about 2 in., and sew securely. On the inside of the finished right end, hand-sew a 2-in.-long piece of the hook side of 1½-in.-wide tape; leave a 2-in. space and add a 5-in.-long piece of the loop side of the tape. To wear the belt, slide the right end through the loop and fasten it underneath.

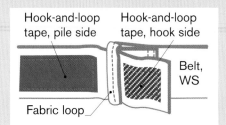

Hook-and-loop tape, pile side

Hook-and-loop tape, hook side

Belt, WS

Fabric loop

decorative stitching on the bezel, if you want. Place the bezel over the shell, position them together on your project, and sew the bezel to the project by hand.

If you're using a bezel fabric that ravels, you'll need to add a ¼-in. seam allowance to the bezel's outer edge also. After stitching the bezel's inner edge through the paper, unthread the needle and stitch again along the outer edge to create a series of holes to serve as a guide for a foldline. Fold the seam allowance of the lower layer under along the holes and baste, then turn the upper seam allowance under.

If the bezel is too tight, warm it with a blow-dryer or light bulb, stretching the Ultrasuede to fit the shell's shape. If it's too loose, run a double-threaded needle through the inner edge and pull up the ends to tighten, then tie the ends securely and bury them inside the bezel.

FOR A QUICK THREAD BEZEL

To create a delicate thread bezel to anchor a small shell, rock, or other find, like the sand dollar on the bag shown at right, use several strands of embroidery floss or other thread. Hold the shell in position while you sew a line of ¼-in.-long buttonhole stitches around it on the fabric. Now sew a second round of buttonhole stitches through and inside the horizontal loops of the first row's stitches. Work the third round the same way, pulling the stitches tight around the shell to hold it in place. Tie off and bury the thread.

You can embellish your design with other small beach finds, drilled or wrapped and sewn in place to create an interesting composition. You'll keep those vacation memories

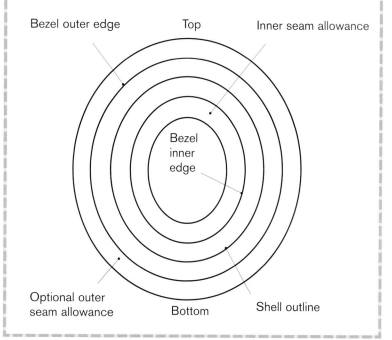

Make a Bezel Pattern

Trace around the seashell, then draw lines about ¼ in. away for both the inner and outer finished edges of the bezel. The inner edge can be a "straight curve" or an undulating line. Mark the shell and bezel at top and bottom. Add a ¼-in. seam allowance to the inner edge, and, if using a fabric that ravels, to the outer edge as well.

Bezel outer edge   Top   Inner seam allowance

Bezel inner edge

Optional outer seam allowance   Bottom   Shell outline

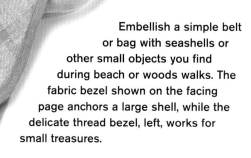

Embellish a simple belt or bag with seashells or other small objects you find during beach or woods walks. The fabric bezel shown on the facing page anchors a large shell, while the delicate thread bezel, left, works for small treasures.

Easy Braided Belts

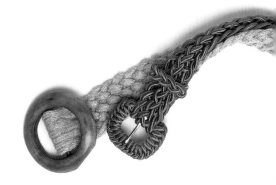

raided belts were always a mystery to me, with their smooth finished tip and—like magic—no visible cut ends. So I did some investigating. Many belts later, I can report that they're not at all difficult to make and, in fact, work up fairly quickly. They can add polish to many outfits, whether you decide to hitch up your jeans with a casual belt from hemp cord, like the natural-colored one shown above, or create a silky smooth version braided from jumbo-weight soutache in a color to coordinate with a silk shirt, like the green belt above.

I'll share two braiding techniques with you that work well for belts: One is a smooth, eight-strand English sennit braid, and the other is similar but with a raised center stitch, called a crocodile ridge. These two styles are variations of a simple over/under braiding technique, using an even number of strands, as shown in the drawings on the facing page. By cutting the strands twice the required length and folding them in half, you eliminate the cut ends at the tip of the belt. This gives a neat finish right where you start. At the other end, you'll attach the strands to a one-piece buckle with or without a prong. If you like, add a simple braided carrier to keep your belt tip from flopping.

PLAY WITH YOUR MATERIALS

It's fun to try a variety of materials for belts, such as jumbo soutache, president's braid, and other pliable braids and cords (I've also tried braiding leather cords but found most to be too stiff for belts). To test a new material, buy a few yards of it, and braid a quick sample belt tip to see how it looks. Also, fold the sample over a buckle to see how thick it will be.

Some materials, such as hemp cord, look great braided, but they create too much bulk at the buckle where several layers meet. One way to reduce this bulk is to pull out any core or filler in the cord before you begin

Tips for Easy Braiding

6-in. by 20-in. piece of foamcore board covered with grid or graph paper makes a good work surface, and sturdy straight- or T-pins work well to hold the braid on the surface. When you reach the bottom of the foamcore, reposition the braid and continue. Use the grid to keep your braiding and the belt's width even, placing pins along the vertical lines. The closer you space the pins, the less the belt will stretch.

If you're using a flat, flexible braid, curve the strand at the braid's outer edges without folding it over. For stiff braids, you'll need to fold the strand at the edge.

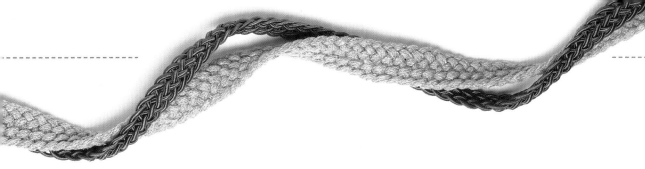

Braiding Strategies

Eight-Strand English Sennit Braid

In hemp cord, this pattern makes a 1¼ in.-wide, 36-in.-long belt..

- 48 ft. of 4-mm braided hemp cord
- 1¼-in.-wide one-piece buckle
- 2-in. piece of matching 1½-in.-wide grosgrain ribbon or Ultrasuede

For belt up to 36 in. long, cut four lengths of hemp cord, each 12 ft. long. For more pliable cord, pull core from each length and discard. Fold each length in half, and pin fold to piece of foamcore board. Arrange strands as shown, and braid following instructions. After each pass, renumber strands from 1 on up, beginning at left before next pass begins.

Starting set-up

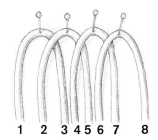

1 2 3 4 5 6 7 8

After passes 1 and 2, with strands renumbered

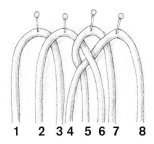

1 2 3 4 5 6 7 8

After pass 8

PASS 1: 6 under 5.

PASS 2: 4 under 5.

PASS 3: Remove pin from fold at tip of 7. 7 over 6, under 5. Pull up to remove excess braid from tip. Pin at center.

PASS 4: 3 over 4, under 5. Pin.

PASS 5: Remove pin from fold at tip of 8.

8 under 7, over 6, under 5; pull up to remove excess braid from tip. Pin at center.

PASS 6: Remove pin from fold at tip of 2. 2 under 3, over 4, under 5. Pull up to remove excess braid from tip. Pin at center.

PASS 7: 8 under 7, over 6, under 5. Pin at center.

PASS 8: Remove pin from fold at tip of 1. 1 over 2, under 3, over 4, under 5. Pull up to remove excess braid from tip. Pin at center.

PASS 9: 8 under 7, over 6, under 5. Pin at center.

PASS 10: 1 over 2, under 3, over 4, under 5. Pin at center.

Repeat passes 9 and 10 for desired length plus 2 in. (3 in. if adding belt carrier).

A great belt is a braid away, using pliable cord and one of two braiding techniques. The belt, above, of natural-colored hemp is braided in the English sennit style; the green soutache braid belt shows the crocodile ridge style.

braiding (this flattens the hemp but doesn't change its look). Another bulk reducer is to stop braiding 1 in. before you reach the buckle, then hand-sew the strands side by side so they'll be flat where they attach. I used both techniques for the hemp belt. Or you can reduce bulk at the buckle by only pulling out and cutting the core before braiding the last 4 in.

A WORD ON LENGTH AND WIDTH

Braided belts are easy to size. The length of a basic belt is your waist measurement plus 5 in. to 6 in. for the tip to slide through the buckle, and 2 in. to fold under where the belt attaches to the buckle (or 3 in. if you want to add a belt carrier). Measure a belt you love to determine the length you want. For a 36-in. belt, I start with 12-ft.-long strands, which will be 6 ft. when folded in half for braiding. In turn, the strands braid down to about half their original length. For a 27-in. belt, start with 9-ft.-long strands. It's better to have a little extra length to work with, and you can simply stop braiding when your belt is the right size.

When choosing a buckle, the width of the belt needs to fit the bar where the belt attaches. Popular belt widths include 1 in., 1¼ in., and 1½ in. To estimate how wide your belt will be, lay eight strands of your braid side by side.

COMPLETING THE BELT

You might want to complete your belt with a braided carrier and braid-covered buckle. A belt carrier is made by simply braiding three strands over and under. Make the carrier twice the width of the belt, plus ¼ in., plus seam allowances. Overlap the ends, stitch them together, and whipstitch the carrier to the belt itself, about 1 in. from the base of the buckle.

To make a matching buckle, cover a plain metal round or oval buckle with the same braid, if it's not too heavy or stiff. Work blanket stitches over the buckle (don't cover the bar). Now you're ready to assemble the belt. Secure the cut ends by machine-stitching across them while squeezing them as close together as possible.

Use a small piece of grosgrain ribbon or Ultrasuede to encase the cut ends and to create a clean finish inside the belt. If you're using a carrier, slip it on the belt, and fold 3 in. of the belt over the bar of the buckle. Push the prong through the center of the braid if the buckle has one. Hand-sew through both layers of the belt on each side of the carrier to hold it in place.

If your belt has no carrier, fold 2 in. of the belt over the buckle's bar, and sew through both layers to secure it. Either way, it's ready to slip on and wear. ●

Eight-Strand Crocodile Ridge Braid

Folding the braid back creates the center ridge. In jumbo soutache, this pattern makes a ⅞-in.-wide belt that's about 36 in. long.

- 48 ft. of jumbo ³⁄₁₆-in. soutache braid
- 1-in.-wide one-piece buckle
- 2-in. piece of matching 1½-in.-wide grosgrain ribbon or Ultrasuede

For belt up to 36 in., cut four lengths of braid each 12 ft. long. Fold each strand in half, and pin at fold to board. Arrange strands as shown, and braid following pattern. After each pass, renumber strands from 1 on up beginning at left before next pass begins.

Starting set-up

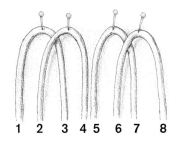

1 2 3 4 5 6 7 8

Pass 2

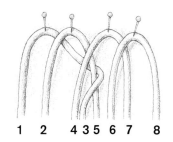

1 2 4 3 5 6 7 8

Pass 3

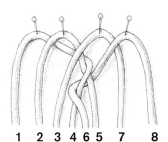

1 2 3 4 6 5 7 8

Pass 4

Pull up strand 1, so loop tightens.

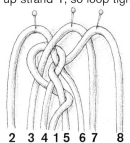

2 3 4 1 5 6 7 8

PASS 1: 4 under 5.

PASS 2: 3 under 4 and 5; fold over 5. Pin fold.

PASS 3: 6 under 5 and 4; fold over 4. Pin fold.

PASS 4: Remove pin from fold at tip of 1. 1 under 2, over 3, under 4 and 5. Pull up to remove excess from tip; fold over 5. Pin fold.

PASS 5: Remove pin from fold at tip of 8. 8 under 7, over 6, under 5 and 4. Pull up to remove excess from tip; fold over 4. Pin fold.

PASS 6: Remove remaining left pin. 1 under 2, over 3, under 4 and 5; fold over 5. Pin fold.

PASS 7: Remove remaining right pin. 8 under 7, over 6, under 5 and 4; fold over 4. Pin fold.

Repeat passes 6 and 7 until belt is 2 in. less than desired length. Weave 4 more inches (5 in. if adding belt carrier) without ridge by taking outside strand under, over, under, over. Alternate sides.

Covered buckle

Work blanket stitch over buckle, pushing stitches close together, so buckle is completely covered. Do not cover bar.

Two Sew-Easy Scarves

The quickest scarf of all: One layer of Polarfleece® plus one seam—does sewing get any easier than this?

Scarves are versatile accessories that I can never have too many of. Whether I turn to my scrap box or indulge in some special fabric, I make piles of them for myself and as gifts. Here are two especially easy, fast methods.

THE EASIEST COWL-NECK SCARF

This accessory is so simple to make that it's almost embarrassing to write about. The reason to write about it is that nearly everyone who's seen the scarf wants one. While the elegant thrift-shop original it was copied from was made from silk, using a single layer of Polartec® 200 transforms the scarf into a warm everyday staple that retains the face-flattering drape of the original. A yard of 60-in.-wide fleece will make three scarves.

Using the pattern on the facing page and placing the fold on the straight grain, cut one layer from double-sided fleece. A rotary cutter with a pinking blade creates a decorative edge (you can also cut with pinking shears or straight scissors). I'd originally planned to sew a line of decorative stitching ¼ in. to ½ in. from all edges, but the finished scarf just didn't need it.

Best of all, this single-layer cowl has only one seam—at the center back. I lapped one pinked edge over the other and joined them with a multistitch zigzag. That's it! Put it on and wear it.

ROLLED-EDGE SCARF

Try hemming all four sides of a gorgeous piece of silk for a quick scarf that would sell for big bucks in a department or specialty store. Use a rolled hemmer foot to get the hems just right.

The tricky part is the corners, and the hardest corner is the last one, according to Cherise Hughes, a custom dressmaker in Fairfield, CT. She shares her expert technique with us: First, pull a thread on each edge and cut so the edge is on grain, which

---

Design **idea**

Elegant Bias Cowl Scarf

*f*or a woven fabric, such as silk, use the same pattern, but cut it on the bias. Sew the center back seam (use a French or flat-felled seam so the inside looks neat), then hem the edges. Alternatively, cut two matching or contrasting pieces. Sew the seam on each, leaving an opening in the middle of one. Then place one inside the other, with the right sides together, and sew around the top and bottom edges. Turn the scarf right side out through the opening in the back seam, and then sew the opening closed by hand. Press lightly.

makes it easier to hem. Use short stitches (12 to 14 per in.) and a small, sharp needle with the 2 mm hemmer for fine silks.

To begin the hem, finger-press the first inch or two by turning it under twice; anchor with a pin. Lower the needle into the roll, take one or two stitches, then lift the foot and coax the fabric edge into the scroll of the foot. Begin stitching.

If the fabric is soft and tends to crush, apply a tiny 1/8-in. by 1/2-in. strip of seam sealant such as Fray Check™ on the edge, blot with a tissue, and roll. This helps when starting a hem and ending the final corner.

Whatever your method, watch the fabric in front of the foot. If you can see the cut edge, it can fall out of the scroll. Guide it into the foot by rolling the edge as it will appear in the finished hem.

When you complete the first side, trim the ends even and start the next edge in the same way. Roll the edge, insert the needle through all layers, and take a stitch, then wiggle the cut edge into the scroll. Tug

gently on the thread ends at the back for a few stitches until the feed dog grips the fabric.

Progress clockwise around the scarf, and at the final corner, use the beginning thread tails to guide the last bit of hem through the foot. Finish the corners by burying the thread ends in the hem for 1 in. to 2 in., then trim. ●

Quick Tip

You can hem a linen napkin using this method and a 4-mm foot, although the corners are trickier on thicker fabric. A lightweight handkerchief linen should work fine.

The rolled hemmer transforms fabric into gorgeous scarves and napkins. With no corners to turn, the top scarf at right is easy—just roll the long sides and fringe the narrow ends. The smokey print scarf at left has four "baby hem" edges. The olive linen napkin hemmed beautifully, but the plaid was too heavy, so we took the easy way out—fringe on all four sides.

A Simple Scarf Pattern

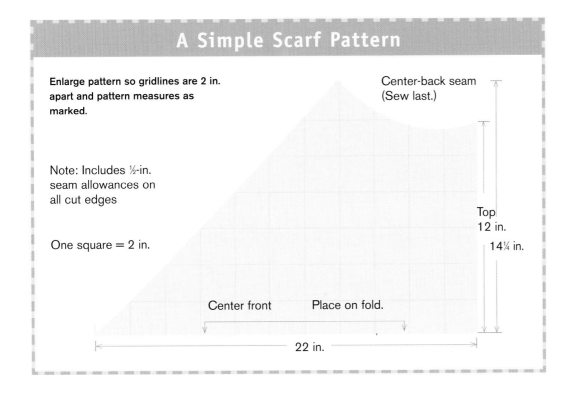

Enlarge pattern so gridlines are 2 in. apart and pattern measures as marked.

Note: Includes 1/2-in. seam allowances on all cut edges

One square = 2 in.

Center-back seam (Sew last.)

Top 12 in.

14 1/4 in.

Center front   Place on fold.

22 in.

Wrap Yourself in Soutache

Make a great belt by joining rows of soutache braid. Zigzagging the rows with invisible thread produces a handsome, textured fabric; an Ultrasuede lining creates a professional finish.

Add a touch of whimsy to a 1-in. striped belt with hand-sewn curls of soutache braid. Make a matching buckle by wrapping a purchased metal buckle with soutache (hint: curved buckles are easier to cover evenly than square ones). Secure cut ends at the back with a few hand stitches and a dot of Fray Check to prevent raveling.

W hile browsing in an elegant New York shop, I noticed a group of fluid belts that appeared to be made from a lustrous ribbed fabric. Upon closer examination, I was delighted to discover that they were made from rows and rows of ordinary rayon soutache braid butted together and sewn.

Of course, I couldn't wait to try the technique for myself, and the belts you see here are the result of my experiments.

Soutache belts aren't difficult to make. With a couple of packages of readily available braid (see Resources on p. 91), fine 0.004-mm nylon monofilament thread, a decorative buckle or a plain one that you cover, and some Ultrasuede or other fabric to use as a lining, you're ready to go. The 1¾-in.-wide belt shown above required about 20 yd. of braid.

You'll join two strands of soutache at a time, gradually building up rows until you reach the width you want.

EASY-BREEZY CONSTRUCTION

To decide on the length of your belt, measure at your waist or hip where you want the belt to sit, and add about 6 in. for overlap and 2 in. for the fold at the buckle end. If you're not sure about the belt's length, model both its length and width after a favorite belt in your wardrobe.

Before diving in, fool around with samples to test the technique and adjust your machine. I used monofilament for the upper thread and bobbin, set my machine on a zigzag 2mm wide and long, and used a machine-embroidery foot with a wide groove on the bottom to accommodate the thickness of the braid.

To "build" the belt, butt the strands of braid firmly together as you guide them under the foot, feeding them evenly so the belt will lie straight. Refer to the sidebar at right to see how to arrange the soutache. After each row, hold the belt up to the light to look for spots where you failed to catch both sides, and resew any gaps.

By stitching in a continuous line around the tip, you'll have to deal with cut ends of braid only at the buckle end, where you can hide them under the lining. The only tricky part is the tip—lay the new strand around the curve with plenty of ease so that the tip will lie flat, and sew slowly. For a smooth curve, stop with the needle down every few stitches to pivot the work. But don't worry if your belt wobbles a bit. After stitching, press it with a press cloth and plenty of steam, and it will flatten nicely.

FINISHING TOUCHES

Once the outer belt is completed, sew a "keeper" (the narrow strip that holds the end of the belt in place) from several strands of soutache braid. They should be long enough to wrap around the belt and overlap about ½ in. on the wrong side. Try on the belt, turn under, and pin the buckle end. (If your buckle has a prong, insert it between strands.) Pin, then hand-sew, the keeper's ends in place.

For a clean lining, cut a strip of Ultrasuede the width of the belt and the finished length minus an inch or two at the buckle end. Pin it to the finished belt back and zigzag around the edges, stopping just shy of the keeper. Finish attaching the Ultrasuede by hand with neat stitches, covering the braid's raw ends.

If your buckle has a prong, use an awl to poke a few smooth, evenly spaced holes in the Ultrasuede so you can close the belt. Alternatively, close it with a strip of hook-

and-loop tape sewn inside the overlap area, or with a couple of hooks and eyes.

After I sewed the first plain belt, I was eager to try one with stripes or braids in contrasting colors. After stitching and pressing the striped base layer, I embellished it with whimsical scrolls of soutache hand-sewn in place; I left this belt unlined.

Of course, you don't have to stick with soutache. You can make a belt from almost any beautiful, straight-edged trim, like metallic tape or twisted cord. A sample will let you know if you're on the right track. ●

An Easy Sewn Belt

Start by zigzagging a doubled length of soutache, then build up the belt by sewing on one new row of braid at a time, wrapping it around one end to create a smooth tip.

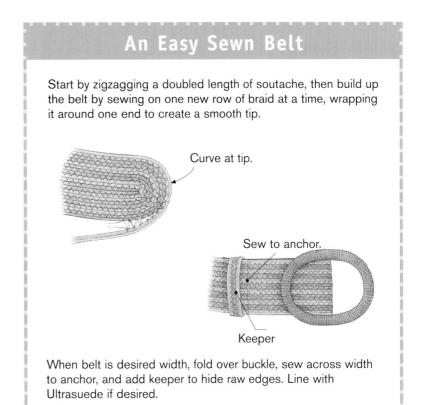

Curve at tip.

Sew to anchor.

Keeper

When belt is desired width, fold over buckle, sew across width to anchor, and add keeper to hide raw edges. Line with Ultrasuede if desired.

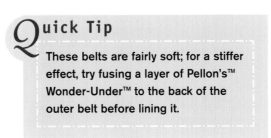

Quick Tip

These belts are fairly soft; for a stiffer effect, try fusing a layer of Pellon's™ Wonder-Under™ to the back of the outer belt before lining it.

Variations On a Shrug

*t*here's no question that a shrug—that frippery of a top that consists of a pair of sleeves and little else—has its place in today's fashion scene. But have you ever considered the practicality of this odd little garment? The shrug has countless uses beyond the traditional evening wrap, including covering bare arms when wearing the ever-fashionable sleeveless dress. Toss one on when indoor air conditioning threatens to make you turn blue, when the sun goes down at a beach party, when you want to feel cozy as you type out that great romance novel, or when you don't want to cover up the front details on a good-looking top or dress with a conventional sweater or jacket.

A shrug makes the proportion of an outfit change completely, with the balance of attention accenting your face and neckline. A shrug offers a terrific way to indulge in higher-priced fabric because you won't need much of it. And best of all, in its simplest version the shrug is easy and quick to sew because it's simply a tube left partly unsewn.

FOR THOSE WHO LOVE FABRIC

There are few fabrics that won't work for shrugs. Those most often pictured in fashion magazines are knits, but it's fun to explore the world of wovens. It seems that the shrug can be made from them all—denim, organza, loosely woven textured wools, soft linens, washed silks, crisp cottons, and even fake

fur. Try luxury fabrics, such as embroidered chiffon, silk brocades, hand wovens, mohair blends, or go for fun fabrics, such as light-hearted rayon prints, gauzy cottons, or parachute nylons and microfibers. Of course, the shrug can always be pieced, decorated with your own specialty embellishment on the cuff and neckline areas, and lined with a contrasting color. The sky is the limit.

Customize a shrug to match your figure and mood. If you have sloping shoulders, try a shrug with set-in sleeves like the crisp plaid taffeta one at left. If you don't want a bare front, make the front section like the shrug shown in the bottom photo on the facing page. And if simplicity is your goal, the velvet shrug in the top photo on the facing page can be made in an hour and looks completely elegant.

THE EASIEST SHRUG

This garment consists simply of a set of sleeves attached across the back. The front can be shaped into a neck opening or left straight and pushed to the back of the neck, creating an attractive curve under the arm.

You can easily sew a tube-style shrug with a rectangle of fabric 24 in. by 45 in. This amount makes a fairly close-fitting shrug with three-quarter sleeves; you'll want to use a larger piece for a looser fit. An oblong scarf can also be used, in which case all you need to do is sew two underarm sleeves (see "Anatomy of a Shrug" on p. 54). The lined

Endless variations on a basic shrug are a cinch to make. Have fun designing your own versions.

Anatomy of a Shrug

A fabric rectangle is all you need to make these shrugs.

For a basic tube shrug, fold fabric in half, join as shown for sleeves, and leave neck/body opening. Use more yardage for fuller sleeves and wider or pieced fabric for longer sleeves.

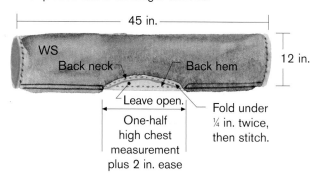

45 in.

12 in.

WS

Back neck

Back hem

Leave open.

Fold under ¼ in. twice, then stitch.

One-half high chest measurement plus 2 in. ease

For a more shaped shrug, cut away front and back necklines.

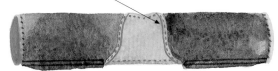

Alternatives for edge-finishing: a serged rolled edge or a bias-bound edge.

For a shrug that closes at center front, cut front neckline straight up from hem.

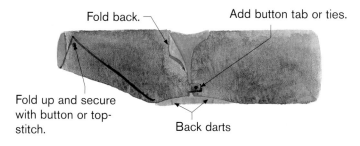

Fold back.

Add button tab or ties.

Fold up and secure with button or top-stitch.

Back darts

To make a shrug from a pattern with set-in sleeves or raglan sleeves, cut the pattern at the bust line.

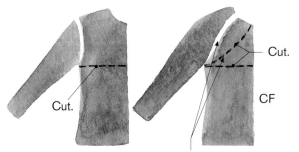

Cut.

Cut.

CF

Use under-sleeve line as neckline, or create a new neckline.

velvet shrug shown in the top photo on p. 52 has a 6-in. slit at the center-back neck to form a turn-back collar. Other than that, it uses the same simple fabric-tube approach.

DETAILS AND REFINEMENTS

The basic shrug can be fine-tuned to suit your style. You can start with a cut-out neckline, and continue to customize by adding a fold-back collar, front and cuff closures, and back darts. If lined, a shrug can be reversible. Details can be incorporated in lots of different combinations: You can experiment with an off-center neckline or pleated shoulders, for example, as shown in the sketches on p. 53.

When using crisper or stiffer fabrics, consider a shrug made with set-in or raglan sleeves. This approach is more time-consuming, and the shrug will look and behave more like a small jacket. Use a pattern that fits you well in the sleeve area—a blouse pattern if you intend to wear it on bare shoulders or a fitted jacket pattern if you want to wear your shrug over another garment. Take a look at "Anatomy of a Shrug" for instructions on adapting a pattern into a shrug.

Finishing details can be as simple as serging the edges or turning them under ¼ in. twice and stitching them down, thus letting the fabric and silhouette carry the design. You can customize a shrug by adding piped edges to the garment's graceful shape, decorative trims, beaded fringe, cuffs, inventive closures, tucks, pleats, or folds (the latter three are especially easy to add if your fabric is 60 in. wide).

So the next time there's a chill in the air, reach for a shrug you've made yourself to stylishly fend it off. Oh, and by the way, shrugs make terrific gifts. ●

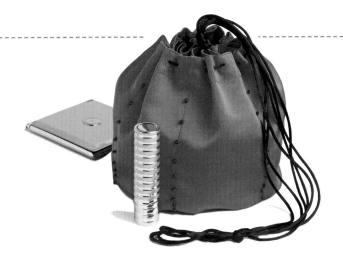

Stitch a Pie Bag

a terrific bag makes life better. Or so it would seem when hunting in the murky depths of a not-so-terrific bag for keys or a pen. A little organization goes a long way in our busy, complicated lives. This little pie bag, with its at-a-glance compartments, keeps your carry-alongs both separated and visible. A simple circle forms the bag's bottom, and three inner walls divide the interior into six pie-shaped sections. If you set the bag down, it doesn't fall over, and its drawstring closure keeps everything snug. Whether for yourself or as a gift, make it as a tote for day, or as an evening handbag by just changing fabric and proportions.

The pie bag is an ideal container for lots of items: storing loose sewing notions, thread, buttons, and unruly ribbons; or corralling socks, lingerie, jewelry, cosmetics, and toiletries for travel. Know an artist? The pie bag is wonderful for storing paints (sew outer pockets for brushes). You get the idea. The pie bag is ultrafunctional. And, of course, it's as easy as you-know-what to sew.

LOOK AT YOUR STUFF

Begin your pie bag by deciding its dimensions. You can vary both the height of the bag and its circumference. You can extend the outer wall above the inner ones, or keep all heights the same. To help you choose dimensions, try out some circles on paper, and imagine the contents inside—do you think they'll fit? Or use the dimensions in the drawings on p. 56 to make a 6-in.-high bag, 11-in. in diameter.

Then draft a pattern for the bag, or measure and cut directly on the fabric (don't forget to add seam allowances). There are only three parts to the pie bag: the bottom, the outer wall, and one pattern piece for the three inner walls. To figure the circumference of the bag, which will determine the length of the outer wall, multiply the diameter of the bottom circle by pi (3.14).

The bag's handy, pie-shaped compartments transport cargo for day or evening. A 10-in.-diameter canvas carryall has added outer pockets (below). The satin evening bag (above) is 5 in. in diameter.

Easy Steps to Make a Pie Bag

The directions below make a bag 6 in. high with an 11 in. diameter. They include ½-in. seam allowances.

STEP 1. Mark and cut fabric as shown. Finish edges. On circle, mark lines on WS from 12 to 6 o'clock, 2 to 8 o'clock, and 10 to 4 o'clock. Stitch in seamline of outer wall to form a tube. Press in ½-in. seam allowance on each end of inner walls.

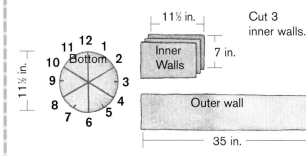

Cut 3 inner walls.

11½ in. — Inner Walls — 7 in.

Outer wall — 35 in. — 7 in.

11½ in.

STEP 2. RSs together, pin, then sew outer wall to bottom.

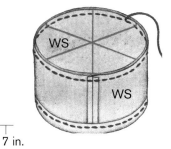

STEP 3. Mark vertical extension lines from bottom on outer wall. Turn RS out.

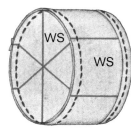

STEP 4. In one continuous seam, stitch inner wall from top of outer wall at 2 o'clock to bottom, pivot, stitch to center bottom, pivot, stitch to 4 o'clock and top of outer wall. Stitch center inner wall from 12 to 6 o'clock. Sew remaining inner wall from 10 to 8 o'clock.

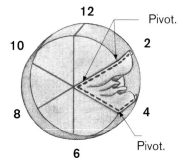

Pivot.

Pivot.

STEP 5. Align inner walls at center, stitch vertical seam to as close as possible to bottom center.

USE NONSTRETCH FABRICS

Since you don't want your bag to sag, work with stable woven fabrics such as lightweight canvas, broadcloth, dupioni, nylon, microfiber, upholstery fabric, leather, and brocades. Avoid knits, challis, crepes, twills, and other fabrics likely to stretch. I like to use lightweight waterproof nylon or good-looking sueded microfiber. The pie bag is unlined, so be sure you like both sides of the fabric you select. Pick up nylon cording to go with your fabric and some grommets in the proper size for the cord.

If your chosen fabric is heavy, use a denim foot on your machine, polyester thread for strength, and a fresh denim or topstitching needle. Otherwise, match thread, needle, and foot to the weight and type of fabric. For light- to medium-weight fabric, I prefer to use the narrow quilter's ¼-in. foot, also known as a patchwork foot, because pivoting the fabric is easier when the needle is visible.

DIVIDING THE PIE

After cutting out the sections for the bag, marking stitching guidelines on the fabric is essential. But first, clean-finish all visible edges. The bags shown here are finished by folding the top edge under twice, then top-stitching. (You may want to skip clean-finishing the edges on the bottom of the bag, though you will see them on the interior when the bag is open or empty.) Add reinforcing topstitching to the top edges, using decorative thread if desired.

Next mark the stitching lines of the compartments onto the wrong side of the bottom of the bag, using a pencil or pen that won't show through to the fabric's right side. After marking, stitch the bottom to the outside wall. Stitch this seam again, $\frac{1}{16}$ in. into the seam allowance, to reinforce the first line of stitching. Now place the bag over one end of the ironing board and extend the guidelines up the outer wall to the top. To sew the rest of the bag, stitch inner walls as shown in the drawing on the facing page.

FINISHING IT OFF

To complete the bag, add eyelets or grommets and cording to make a drawstring closure and carrying handle. Although you can machine-stitch buttonholes or eyelets, I recommend using grommets, because the cord will slide through them easily, and they'll hold up to lots of abrasion. They're easy to install if you buy them in a kit at your notions store. Reinforce the grommet area with a small square of self-fabric.

Using a slippery nylon cord makes it easy to loosen the knot used to close the bag. However, it's okay to use other materials for the cording, like ribbon or smooth yarn. You'll need three generous lengths of cording (try 1 yd. each), then follow the suggested threading sequences in the drawings, or invent your own way to tie the bag.

The nylon beach bag above is 11 in. in diameter and 13 in. high.

While you're inventing, try some design variations using the pie-bag concept. Simply changing the proportions will result in a different-looking bag. Embellish: add tassels, buttons, or trim, or quilt it. Whether you make it humble and utilitarian, or snazz it up for evening, I hope you'll agree that the pie bag takes the cake. ●

Attach Grommets and Cord

Make sure grommets are large enough to allow cord to pass easily.

Evenly space grommets as shown, attaching with grommet tool. Cut three lengths of cord, knot, and thread as in the diagram.

Knot center loops.

Overstitched Bags and Portfolios

esigner Bird Ross doesn't know me, but she has strongly influenced my life. After reading about her inventive quilted garments, I began to overstitch everything that wasn't nailed down, including the portfolio and handbags on these pages.

These projects are fun, expressive, and quick. Perhaps they'll turn you into an overstitcher, too.

JUSTIFY THAT FABRIC STASH

This project defends your need to maintain a, shall we say, voluminous inventory of fabrics. You'll need three fabrics for the main piece —
an outer fabric, filler, and lining—and as many as four additional fabrics for trims. You'll also need a variety of contrasting threads and a length of sew-in Velcro. If you're making a purse, you'll want nylon webbing for the strap or, for a portfolio, braid or ribbon for ties. You can adjust the dimensions of the patterns for the size you desire. All the sewing is straight stitching.

For the outer layer, try a lightweight, flexible fabric, like drapey rayon, cotton chintz, or raw silk. Craft felt works well for the filler, while the inside can be anything from sandwashed silk to polyester lining fabric.

READY, CUT, STITCH, WASH

Stack and rough-cut the three body fabrics, adding 3 in. to each edge to allow for shrinkage during stitching and laundering. Pin the layers together every few inches.

For overstitching, use a straight stitch to sew giant zigs and zags, reversing every 4 in. to 6 in. by using the machine's reverse setting. Cover the surface with at least 25 angled rows, then change thread colors and stitch again in the opposite direction.

Throw the piece into the washer and dryer, then press. The piece will lose its shape, become wrinkled, and shrink, but that's just the effect you want. Finally, stitch the surface with a third thread color, concentrating on the areas you missed before. Wash, dry, and iron again.

Portfolio

Rough-cut 27 in. by 36 in.

Tie

12 in.

6 in.

Top flap

Velcro

9 in.

9 in.

Side flap

Bottom flap

Trim to 21 in. by 30 in., then cut out corners.

FINISHING TOUCHES

Trim the piece to fit your pattern (removing corners to create flaps for the portfolio). Then select from the following finishing options.

Add appliqué

Fuse appliqué shapes to the outside of your piece using Pellon's Wonder-Under. Stitch them—and any ribbons or trims—in place with giant zigs and zags. I left a 2-in. unstitched section in the portfolio's striped ribbon for a business card.

Triangle-trim edges

For a textured edge with a sawtooth finish like that on the portfolio, select a fabric for the trim and cut a 2-in. square for every 1½ in. of raw edge (the portfolio took 55 squares). Starting at a corner, fold a square over the edge and pin, then add the next square, overlapping by about 1 in. Continue around the perimeter, neatly folding the squares at the corners. When all the squares are pinned in place, zig and zag over them, then reverse direction and repeat with a new thread color.

To complete the portfolio, tack two lengths of braid or ribbon to the inside, as shown in the drawing on the facing page, leaving the ends loose. Place a piece of mat board in the center and your papers on top, then tie to anchor them. Fold in the side flaps, then the bottom and top, fastening the last two flaps with squares of Velcro.

Smooth bar edges

For the smooth, straight edges shown on the bags, select three to four fabrics and cut them in 2-in.-wide strips. To begin, attach a "pull" on each side for opening the bag. To make a pull, cut a 2-in. by 10-in. strip, fold the long edges to meet at the center, then fold in half again. Overstitch the strip, cut it in half, and fold as shown in the drawing

When finished, the portfolio on the facing page will measure 9 in. by 12 in. The dimensions of the shoulder bags, above, are 8½ in. by 17 in.

below. Then baste each loop in place on the bag, 1 in. from the top.

Using a different fabric to finish each top edge, fold a 2-in. strip in half and pin over the edge, with the strip's raw edges exposed, then overstitch. Cut 1-in.-wide Velcro the bag's length, pin half inside each top edge, and anchor with stitching.

Repeat the same trim on the side edges, turning in the strip's short cut ends, and overstitch. Then cut a 70-in. length of webbing for the shoulder strap and insert it between the sides before folding the bag and overstitching to join all the layers. Voilà! Your bag is finished. ●

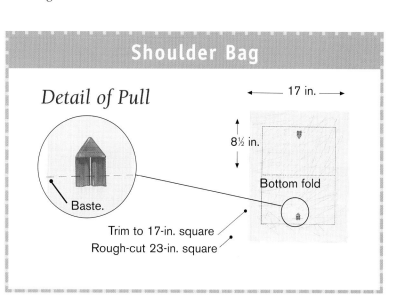

Shoulder Bag

Detail of Pull

Baste.

17 in.

8½ in.

Bottom fold

Trim to 17-in. square
Rough-cut 23-in. square

The Simplest Summer Skirt

Make it single-layer for a bathing-suit cover-up, or double the layers for a more opaque, wear-everywhere warm-weather staple.

One of my longtime-favorite garments is a pair of summer pants made from silk chiffon in a softly rumpled, indigo blue print. With a pull-on waist and no pockets, these pants couldn't be simpler, yet they're wonderfully versatile to wear. So, I decided, why not make an elegantly comfortable skirt along the same lines? Whether you wear this skirt over a swimsuit at a pool party, as shown at left, or with a mid-thigh-length, silky cotton tunic for dinner, I think you'll find that, dressed up or down, it feels elegant and just right.

If you find a single layer of chiffon too sheer to be practical, you can wash the fabric by hand so it crinkles and becomes more opaque (then iron it lightly); wear it over lightweight cotton leggings; or line it with a second, complementary fabric. Combining two solid or print chiffons can give interest-ing and varied results that are still delicate, as shown on the facing page.

And if you tend to avoid gathered skirts because of their unflattering bulk at the waist and hip, you don't need to worry about that problem with this skirt—the fine chiffon crushes down to virtually nothing, even when you gather yards of fabric into the waist.

CHIFFON—GO FOR REAL SILK!

If you've been a bit leery of sewing with silk chiffon, this skirt is a perfect first project. If you turn a 3-yd. length of fabric sideways, as I did, you have to sew only one seam, fold the selvage under at the waist, stitch to form a casing for strips of elastic, then hem the skirt. That's it. This is truly one skirt you can sew today and wear tonight (why do they always say that, when it's seldom true?), and it'll look like you spent $250 to buy it.

You'll find lots of different qualities of chiffon in stores. Please don't try to save money with a synthetic chiffon—it'll be hot and sticky, it won't press or drape well, and

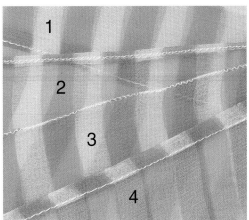

Take your pick from several delicate hem options. From top, for a sporty finish, press under ¼ in., then 1 in., and stitch close to the top fold (1); use the narrow, double-turned hem to get the prettiest results (2); try a single row of narrow zigzagging, then trim close to it for an easy hem (3); or use the hemmer foot to make a quick, narrow hem (4).

the seams will pucker. So stick with silk. You'll find that some silk chiffons are finely woven and sheer, like the French striped fabric I used for my skirt on the facing page, while others from India have a coarser, homespun quality resembling gauze and still others are nearly opaque. The one you choose depends on the type of skirt you want. I think stripes look cool and summery, but the skirt would be equally gorgeous in one of the iridescent, solid-color chiffons.

MINIMAL CONSTRUCTION NEEDED

I've outlined just how easy the skirt is to make. For supple seams and the most beautiful finish, I suggest sewing the skirt with 100-weight silk thread and a fine, size 60/8 or 70/10 needle. For the single vertical seam, try a short (2 mm) straight stitch, then a narrow and short (1 mm wide and long) zigzag just next to it. To avoid puckering, sew the seam on a ⅜-in. seam allowance, then trim the excess fabric close to the stitching. Starting at the waist end of the seam, sew for ¼ in., leave a 1-in. opening for inserting the elastic, then sew the rest of the seam.

Turning the fabric sideways allows you to use the fabric's selvage edge for a quick, clean finish inside the waistband. Fold under 1¼ in. at the waist; stitch twice around, at 1 in. and ½ in. from the fold; and insert a length of ⅜-in.-wide elastic into each opening you've created in the casing.

If you're making a two-layer skirt and want it to be reversible, sew the vertical seam on each layer separately, leaving one seam open as described for inserting the elastic, then place the layers right sides together and stitch at the waist. Press and turn, then stitch as explained above to form casings for the elastic, which you'll insert between the two layers. Hem the layers separately to achieve maximum "float."

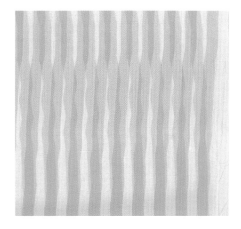

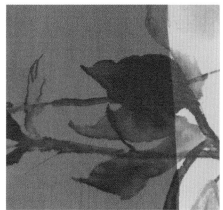

You can finish the hem of your skirt in any number of ways. For a sporty finish, turn the hem up twice to form a 1-in.- to 1¼-in.-wide hem and stitch near the top fold, as shown in sample 1 in the photo on the facing page. You can use a hemmer foot to create a narrow baby hem (sample 4); or turn, stitch, trim, turn, and stitch again, for the neatest ⅛-in. hem (sample 2); as I did on my skirt. Perhaps the easiest hem is a simple zigzag, about 1.5 mm wide and 0.7 mm long (not quite a satin stitch, but almost), sewn ¼ in. or more from the edge, then trimmed close to the stitching (sample 3). Experiment with scraps of fabric until you find the hem that you like best.

And that's it. Put on your skirt, and wear it again and again and again. And you thought fine sewing had to be complicated! ●

Layering two silk chiffons reduces sheerness and creates interesting effects. From top left, two layers of the green stripe give an energetic, shadow-box effect; layering the narrow yellow/white stripe under the green stripe turned sideways yields playful results; a woven shadow stripe looks neat over the yellow/white stripe, with the stripes heading in different directions; a layer of ombré chiffon adds subtle color to a minimalist watercolor print.

The best home-decorating gifts are those that are practical as well as attractive. We think they should be luxurious, fun, and a little whimsical as well. In the following pages you'll find directions for making customized clothes hangers, a pincushion in the shape of a dress form, fanciful pillows, and scaled down quilting projects. And as a finishing touch, there are two types of intriguing and beautiful gift boxes that will be treasured as much as any gift you place inside. They're quick to make; so be sure to make a few to keep on hand. ●

part 4

Home
Accessories

Embroidered Felt Trivets

*r*ecently I found a fascinating collection of vintage wool-felt trivets and coasters at a flea market. They were all different shapes and adorned with lively, yet simple, embroidery. Geometric shapes—circles, triangles, half-moons, and stars—were cut out of the trivets, leaving holes that had been outlined with contrasting whipstitches.

I was instantly inspired. How could I make a modern version of these lovely antiques? The resulting trivets not only reflect my love of graphic forms and delicate embroidery, but also are functional. I'll show

you how to make your own versions, which I think you will find easy, fun, and also creatively satisfying.

MATERIALS

Wool felt is wonderful—dense, yet thin, with a smooth, soft surface. But it's hard to find pure wool felt, or even blends. So I made these trivets with readily available acrylic felt, which worked fine. Later, however, I found terrific places to get real wool felt in loads of colors and weights (see Resources on p. 91).

Besides a supply of felt in colors you love, you'll need cotton embroidery thread, wood glue, and a package of ³⁄₃₂-in.-thick cork (available at hardware stores) to use as backing to protect your furniture.

The cork backing is my addition to the vintage design, and to keep the cork from showing through the cut-out shapes, I layered other colors of felt beneath them. Not

only do the additional layers protect your tabletops from hot dishes, but they can also provide more opportunities to design with color.

DESIGN AND CONSTRUCTION

I find inspiration for trivet designs just about everywhere, but flipping through magazines is a quick way to find interesting patterns and shapes. Imagine your patterns and shapes in layers of color, then, using a sharp pencil and a ruler, draw the designs on ¼-in. graph paper. Plan the pattern shapes for each color of over- or underlay. Enlarge or reduce your drawings on a photocopier if you like. Cut out, or trace onto another piece of paper and cut out, to create templates for cutting felt.

Before assembling your trivets, you may want to prepare your felt first. If you are using acrylic felt, take these steps to eliminate the "frizzies" that often accompany it and could obscure your embroidery work. First, preshrink the felt in hot water and dry

Graphic possibilities of shape and color are endless with felt trivets. Add embroidery stitches and a cork backing, and you've got a festive note to add to a table. Smaller versions make terrific coasters.

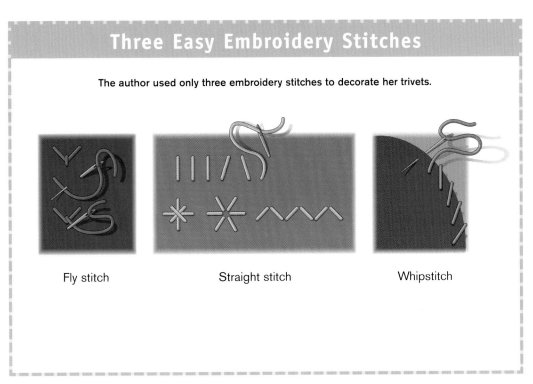

Three Easy Embroidery Stitches

The author used only three embroidery stitches to decorate her trivets.

Fly stitch   Straight stitch   Whipstitch

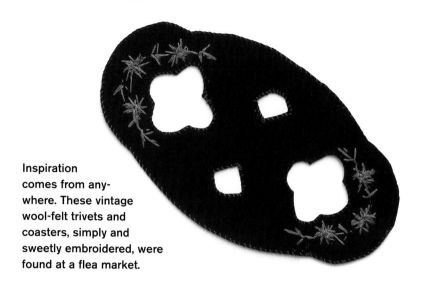

Inspiration comes from anywhere. These vintage wool-felt trivets and coasters, simply and sweetly embroidered, were found at a flea market.

Design idea

Make a Felt Trivet or Coaster

these basic instructions for creating felt trivets or coasters are flexible—adjust the layering order so it makes sense to you. Sometimes a complete underlayer works well (for example, when there are lots of cutouts with the same color felt behind them); other times it makes more sense to patch smaller pieces under a larger shape. For the embroidery stitches, experiment with using three or six strands of embroidery floss. Some colors have less impact than others and stand out better with more strands.

STEP 1. Prepare your design and felt as described on p. 65.

STEP 2. Cut out all the pieces of felt, and choose the largest pattern for the base.

STEP 3. Pin, baste, or fuse the overlay shapes in place on the felt base piece.

STEP 4. Whipstitch the overlays in place with embroidery floss, working from the center out.

STEP 5. Whipstitch the underlayer sections on the trivet's back, using a matching color of sewing thread.

STEP 6. Outline the underlayer shapes as well as the perimeter of the trivet with whipstitches, using embroidery floss in contrasting colors. Embroider additional decorative stitches as desired.

STEP 7. Mist the back of the trivet, then iron dry. Do the same for the front of the trivet.

STEP 8. Cut the cork ⅛ in. smaller than the outside perimeter of the trivet.

STEP 9. Use wood glue to bind the cork to the back of the trivet.

it in the dryer. Then mist the dried felt with water and iron it dry. Ironing acrylic felt usually causes the felt to melt, shrink, and stick to your iron, but preshrinking the felt eliminates this problem.

Frizzies are not a big problem if you are using 100 percent wool felt or a blend of wool and rayon. But these fibers will also benefit from the preshrinking process.

Follow the steps outlined in the sidebar and on p. 65 to assemble and embroider your trivets. That's it. These sturdy, functional examples of your design and embroidery skills will liven up your dining table or serve as delightful coasters to sprinkle about your home. ●

Pillow and Pyramid Gift Boxes

*t*he best presents come in beautiful little boxes—or so the saying goes. These pillow and pyramid boxes are the perfect wrapping for small gifts. They can be made from paper or fabric, and either left plain or embellished with ribbons, buttons, beads, or baubles. You can make boxes that are simple or fancy, silly or sophisticated—whatever fits the occasion and the gift. And most of the materials you'll need may already be lurking in your collection of sewing and craft supplies, although you may want to purchase some special papers for these boxes.

To make fabric-covered boxes, laminate light- to medium-weight woven fabrics to printmaking paper, which is about as thick as a greeting card or file folder. Quilting cottons, novelty prints, rayons, and silk are excellent fabric choices. You can use any of the fusible webs available to bond the fabric and paper. Following the directions that come with the fusible web, iron it to your fabric's wrong side first, then fuse the fabric to the paper.

Paper and fabric-covered boxes make the perfect wrapping for little gifts such as sewing notions, jewelry, and gift certificates.

STICKY STUFF AND PAPER

This project requires three kinds of adhesive: glue stick to make the box templates, fusible web to laminate the fabric to paper, and quick-drying Designer Tacky Glue to finish the boxes. (See Resources on p. 91 for this and other supplies mentioned here.) Of the many beautiful papers available, printmaking papers designated 90-lb. to 140-lb. weight are ideal for both plain and fabric-covered boxes and hold their shape well. Also consider using highly textured papers with a handmade look, some of which have the added beauty of embedded flowers and leaves.

ONE SIZE FITS ALMOST ALL

For small to medium pyramid boxes, you need only draw one template for each type of box. You can photocopy the patterns, then enlarge each template on a photocopier to a variety of sizes. To make large boxes, elongate a medium-large box rather than enlarging the whole box. You can make pillow and pyramid boxes in any size, provided the paper you use is heavy enough to maintain the box's shape. To make permanent templates, glue the template copies to thin poster board using a glue stick and cut them out along the outside lines (but don't cut the scoring lines). For accurate, sharp inside corners, cut from the box's outside edges in toward each corner. By accurately measuring and cutting your templates, you can ensure that each box will fold into a perfect shape.

EASIER THAN FALLING OFF A LOG

Once your templates are prepared, you'll be able to complete a box in five to ten minutes. With a well-sharpened pencil or extra-fine-point marking pen, trace the pattern's cutting lines (but not the foldlines) onto the paper's wrong side (whichever side you want to be inside the box). Then cut the box out along the drawn lines. (Don't cut the slits for the tabs in the pyramid box just yet.)

Using a Hera™ fabric marker or a letter opener, and the edge of a ruler as your guide, score the foldlines. Consult your template to determine their placement, and press firmly as you draw. Use the pillow-box template on the facing page to make scoring the curved lines a painless operation.

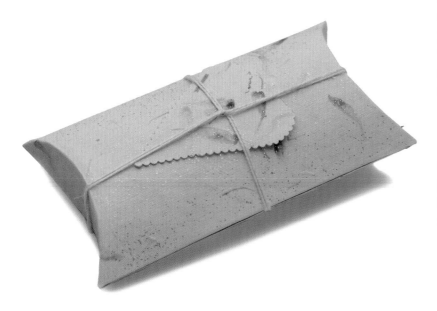

FOLD, SEAL, AND DELIVER

Fold all scored lines (on both types of box) toward the inside, creasing each foldline individually. When all the lines are firmly set, fold the box into its final shape.

Pillow box pops into shape

Fold the pillow box in half along its center line, fold the tab inward, and apply a thin coat of quick-drying glue to the tab's right side to glue the box's sides together. Lay the box between two sheets of wax paper and weigh it down with a heavy book until the glue has thoroughly dried. Turn in the box's ends along the curved foldlines while gently squeezing the box on its sides, and it will pop into shape.

Ties or tabs close the pyramid box

With all four sides folded up to form the pyramid shape, check the positions of the tabs and marked slots. Redraw the slots if needed to properly align them with tabs A and B, then cut the slots with a craft knife. Fold flaps C and D to the inside, and glue them in place. (If you are using very thick papers, you can cut the flaps off if you prefer.)

For a pyramid box that ties closed, glue string or ribbon in place under the flaps on sides C and D. To close the box, fold sides A and B to the inside, slip the tabs into their slots, then tie the remaining sides. Or, to close the box using the tabs only, fold sides C and D to the inside first, then slip the tabs into their slots.

Once you've made just a few of these beautiful boxes, you'll begin to create the boxes first, and then look for items to fill them. Just be careful that the box doesn't outshine the gift! •

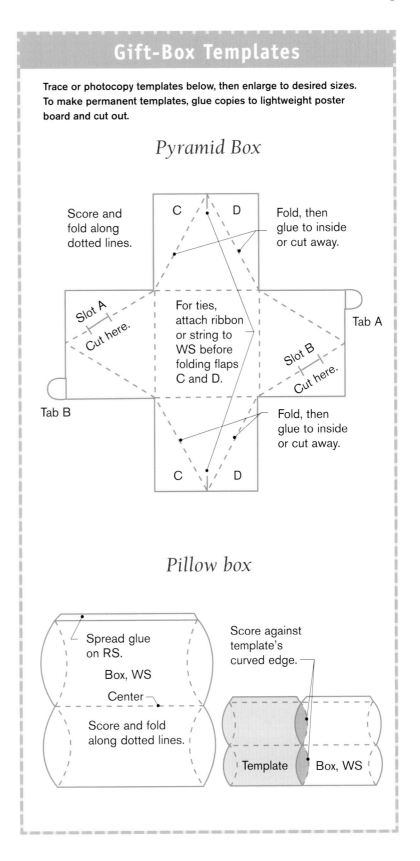

Gift-Box Templates

Trace or photocopy templates below, then enlarge to desired sizes. To make permanent templates, glue copies to lightweight poster board and cut out.

Pyramid Box

Score and fold along dotted lines.

C   D

Fold, then glue to inside or cut away.

Slot A
Cut here.

For ties, attach ribbon or string to WS before folding flaps C and D.

Tab A

Slot B
Cut here.

Tab B

Fold, then glue to inside or cut away.

C   D

Pillow box

Spread glue on RS.

Box, WS

Center

Score and fold along dotted lines.

Score against template's curved edge.

Template   Box, WS

A Pillow from Neckties

Wait—don't toss those gorgeous old neckties! Recycle the points to create a unique and richly textured pillow. The 14-in. red pillow requires about 35 tie points, while you can make the framed blue pillow with just 14.

*i*f you love beautiful fabrics, it just makes sense to collect men's neckties that have gone out of style—those gorgeous silks are too wonderful to throw out. But most of the projects I've seen that recycle ties end up discarding the points. That's why I've developed a couple of pillows made almost entirely from leftover necktie points.

I got the idea when my neighbor's house was getting a new roof. My arrangement of necktie points on a base layer of fabric resembles roofing shingles or fish scales, with each row covering the stitching of the row beneath. And since silk neckties are fully lined, the points are cleanly finished and ready to use—all you have to do is trim them off about 3½ in. from the tip.

A large collection of ties gives you the luxury of playing with color. But it's possible to create an interesting pillow from just 14 tie points, like that shown at left above. You can sort your collection of points into color families and work with many variations of a single color, like my pillows above. Your design can be totally random, or you can "paint" with color, arranging the points in a layout that pleases you before you begin to sew them down. Sometimes, the uglier the ties, the more exciting the pillow! Once you start, you'll find that these pillows are truly quick to make and yield gorgeous results.

Each pillow cover has a velvet back with a zipper, so it's easy to remove for cleaning. I suggest that you dry-clean the completed pillow, since the points don't wash or press well.

ROUNDING UP MATERIALS

The fact that a tie has two pointed ends, one large and one small, increases your design options: You can mix the small and large ends together in a pillow for a varied effect, or stick with just one size throughout. When a new tie enters my studio (either from my thrift-shop searches or from friends who know I love them), I immediately open the tie seam, remove the interfacing, press, and cut off the points, using the measurements in the drawing on the facing page, then add them to my stash.

I used a 14-in.-square pillow insert, but you can easily adapt the design for other sizes and shapes. Aside from the ties, you'll need black cotton for the base fabric and a piece of fleece the same size. (I used a 15-in. square for the red pillow and 9½-in. square for the blue one; I prefer Quilter's Fleece #989 from Pellon.) You'll also need two 8½-in. by 15-in. pieces of velvet for the pillow back, and a 14-in. zipper. For the blue pillow style, choose a stable, coordinating fabric for the border, like my prequilted, iridescent taffeta; a 14-in. pillow requires four 3¾-in. by 16-in. pieces. To fill in the spaces between the bottom row of tie points, you'll need a few assorted tie fabrics, three 4-in. by 5½-in. pieces for the red pillow, and two 4-in. by 5-in. pieces for the blue.

FISH-SCALE CONSTRUCTION

To make a pillow covered with tie points, first mark the base fabric as shown in the drawing, sew the "background" fabrics for the first row of tie points, then add the points one row at a time. When the front is complete, assemble the back, inserting the zipper between the velvet pieces using a 1-in. seam allowance and lapping the top edge over the zipper an extra ¼ in. so it doesn't "grin" when the pillow is finished.

With right sides together and the zipper flap pointing toward the bottom, pin and stitch the pillow front to the back in a ½-in. seam. If you're adding twisted cord to the pillow edges, as I did, leave a 1-in. opening at the bottom center for finishing the cord ends.

To attach the cord, either slipstitch it in place by hand, or butt the cord to the pillow and machine-zigzag it with invisible thread, easing in extra cord around the corners. Either way, insert the cord ends into the opening you left in the pillow, and sew by hand to anchor them.

FRAMED-PILLOW BASICS

Construction for the blue pillow is similar but requires fewer tie points, sewn on four marked lines. When the center section is complete, match the center of one border piece to the center of one side of the center section, and stitch to within ½ in. of each corner. Repeat for the other three sides. To create a miter, fold and crease the border fabric diagonally, check the alignment, and then open and stitch the corner. Trim the excess fabric, press lightly, and then add the pillow back, as for the red pillow.

Of course, you don't have to limit your creativity to pillows! Try inserting smaller sections of tie points into seams and borders for a great zigzag edge, like prairie points. How about a vest or a little tie-point bag? Or use larger tie points at the edge of a window valance or bed cover. ●

Tie-Pillow Tactics

It's easy to recycle necktie points to create a beautiful pillow. Experiment to find a pleasing arrangement before you begin stitching.

Tie-Point Schematic for Larger End

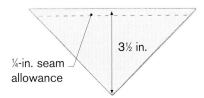

STEP 1. For allover design, draw six lines on base fabric as shown (for inset design, draw bottom four rows only). Layer and baste fleece to WS.

STEP 2. Join underlay pieces on short ends, press seams to one side, and sew strip at bottom line, matching raw edges.

STEP 3. Starting at lower left, arrange first row of tie points on bottom line, overlapping pieces and placing points ½ in. from bottom. Trim excess at side edges. Stitch in ¼-in. seam, then zigzag over raw edges. Repeat on subsequent rows, making sure points cover base fabric and stitching, and staggering points for interesting arrangement.

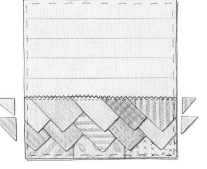

STEP 4. Baste raw edges at pillow sides. Pin up lower row of points so they won't be caught in seam. Front is ready for pillow assembly.

Great Pillows 1,2,3

*f*eaturing classic button details and an intriguing contrast of translucent silk organza and earthy, textured linen and silk, these three easy-to-sew pillows resemble the $200 variety available from fine stores and interior designers, but at a much lower price. You don't need a lot of fabric for these pillows, so purchase the best—while silk organza adds polish, the polyester version doesn't press well.

PLEATED "APRON" PILLOW

The elegant, pleated-organza apron flap on this linen pillow (shown at left in the photo below) looks hard to make but isn't. Start with a 16-in.-square pillow form. I prefer the cushiness of down or a feather/down blend, but you can also use a polyester form (see Resources on p. 91).

Follow the construction details in the drawings on the facing page to complete the front, back, tab, and apron flap, using a ½-in. seam allowance.

Fragile silk organza contrasts with rough linen and "scribbled" China silk to create stunning pillows for your home. From left, a pleated "apron" pillow, a handwritten silk pillow in a sheer "envelope," and a long rectangle with three organza "pinafores" and double-button trim.

Apron Pillow

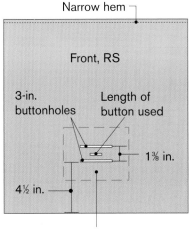

Narrow hem

Front, RS

3-in. buttonholes

Length of button used

1⅜ in.

4½ in.

Fuse interfacing on WS.

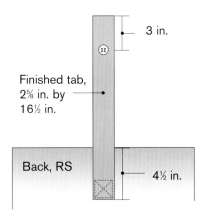

3 in.

Finished tab, 2⅝ in. by 16½ in.

Back, RS

4½ in.

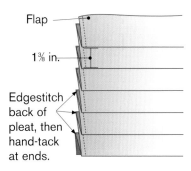

Flap

1⅜ in.

Edgestitch back of pleat, then hand-tack at ends.

STEP 1. Cut 17-in. square of linen for both front and back. Finish top edge with narrow hem. Fuse interfacing behind buttonhole area and machine-sew buttonholes on front before assembling.

STEP 2. To make tab, start with 5½-in. by 17½-in. rectangle. Fold it lengthwise, RSs together. Stitch long side and one end. Trim, turn, and press. Then turn open end to inside and press. Attach tab to center of back by stitching box with X inside, as shown, over open end.

STEP 3. Cut organza flap 17 in. by 25½ in. and finish side and lower edges with narrow hem. Draw chalk lines every 2¾ in., starting ½ in. from top raw edge. Use 1⅜-in.-wide oaktag template on marked line to fold and press each of six pleats. Edgestitch back of each pleat, then hand-tack in place at side hems.

To assemble the pillow, baste the pleated flap to the top of the pillow back, right sides together. Join the front and the back, right sides together, stitching side and bottom edges (lift the flap away from the back so you don't sew it into the side seam). When stitching the lower corners, taper as shown in the bottom drawing on p. 75. Now stitch the flap to the back's top edge. Serge the seam allowances together, press to back, and topstitch. Slip the pillow into the case, then slipstitch the linen front and back together at the top opening to prevent gaping. The flap will cover the top edge of the pillow. Attach a beautiful button to the tab to close it. Why not use a great vintage button?

A "LETTER AND ENVELOPE"

This fun pillow (shown at center in the photo on the facing page), inspired by one made by Pennington Home of Dallas, TX, is essentially a fabric letter. The 8-in. by 12½-in. inner pillow of China silk is covered with words handwritten in fine-point permanent

Pinafore Pillow

Cut organza in 7-in. squares, press under 1-in. edge all around using oaktag template, and refold corners diagonally as shown to create a miter shadow. Center and pin squares to linen front, and satin-stitch each square to pillow, covering raw edge beneath and using wide, short zigzag. On each side of square, end stitching with needle on right, then pivot and stitch next side. Sew buttons (stack two together) at center of each square.

Completed miter

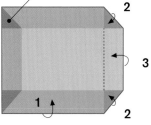

STEP 1. To create miter, after pressing under 1-in. edges, fold edge.

STEP 2. Fold corner diagonally.

STEP 3. Fold edge.

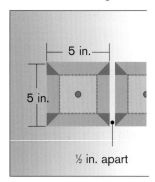

5 in.

5 in.

½ in. apart

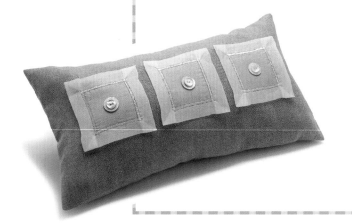

marker, which can convey any message you like. (My handwritten quotes are from an old book on fabrics.)

For this odd size, you'll need to make a muslin pillow form, lightly filling it with fiberfill (you want it fairly flat). After writing your "letter" on the China-silk fabric, sew a simple pillow cover, insert the pillow into it, and slipstitch the opening closed.

The delicate outer cover is a silk-organza envelope, constructed as shown in the top drawing on the facing page. I sewed mine a bit larger than the inner pillow, since the

extra roominess exaggerates its fragility. The envelope is easy to make—just narrow-hem the edges as shown, then stitch sides together in a ¼-in. seam using a narrow zigzag. Add a button to the top flap and one to the envelope's lower V; tie a piece of silk ribbon to the top button to wrap in a figure eight around the two buttons. Voilà, an envelope.

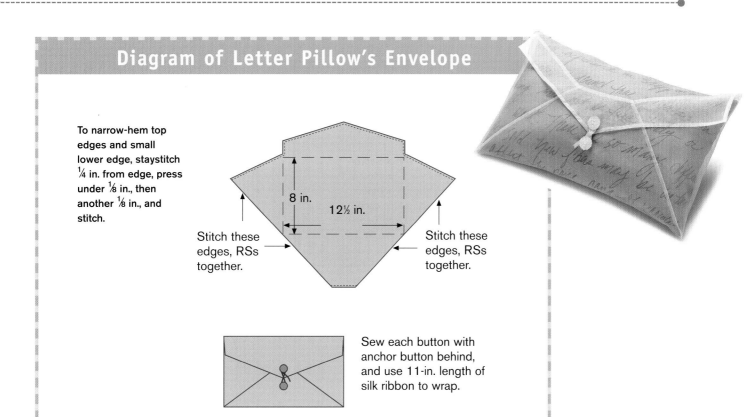

To narrow-hem top edges and small lower edge, staystitch ¼ in. from edge, press under ⅛ in., then another ⅛ in., and stitch.

8 in.

12½ in.

Stitch these edges, RSs together.

Stitch these edges, RSs together.

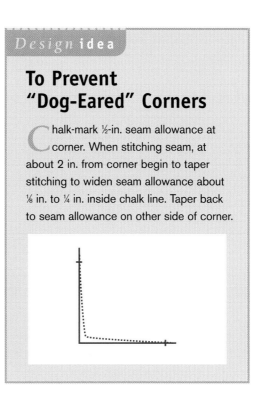

Sew each button with anchor button behind, and use 11-in. length of silk ribbon to wrap.

EASY "PINAFORE" PILLOW

It's simple to embellish a plain linen pillow with three square, silk-organza "pinafores" (as shown at right in the photo on p. 72). Construct the squares as shown on the facing page; a 1-in.-wide oaktag template helps in evenly pressing under the edges. Satin stitch the squares to a linen pillow front 12 in. by 21 in. (its finished size will be 11 in. by 20 in.); Sulky rayon thread in a slightly lighter or darker shade than the organza works well. Assemble the pillow in the usual way, tapering the corners as shown to prevent dog-ears.

And that's it. Have fun inventing your own new pillow designs. ●

Design **idea**

To Prevent "Dog-Eared" Corners

Chalk-mark ½-in. seam allowance at corner. When stitching seam, at about 2 in. from corner begin to taper stitching to widen seam allowance about ⅛ in. to ¼ in. inside chalk line. Taper back to seam allowance on other side of corner.

Ribbonwork Holiday Stocking

A ribbonwork stocking is ready in a snap, and this construction method eliminates raw edges on both the outside and inside.

a visit to an incredible ribbon shop in San Francisco, named after its owner, Paulette Knight, triggered my interest in the time-honored art of ribbonwork. Inspired by the store's small samples of basket-woven ribbons, I made a ribbonwork runner for a dining table, then a vest, and finally a series of holiday stockings like the one above.

For the stocking shape, I used a commercial pattern, removed the seam allowances, and made a tagboard template of the shape. You can use luscious ribbons of any width and material, from hand-dyed silk to sheers, metallics, iridescent taffeta, velvet, satin, bias-cut fabric, and even wired ribbon if you remove the wire. If you can't find ribbon in just the color you want, try layering a sheer

silk or metallic over another ribbon (press sheers and metallics to see if they can withstand an iron's heat). You'll need about 16 yd. total for a plain-weave front on a stocking 7½ in. wide by 15 in. long. I used five different ribbons for my stocking, about 4 yd. of three and 2 yd. of the other two. But buying a little extra ribbon allows you some options with other weaving patterns.

You'll also need a blocking board. I made one with a plywood base topped with an ironing-board pressing pad and a layer of cotton duck cloth, but June Tailor offers a nicely sized Pin-Weave Express Board. Also required are a stable, lightweight, fusible interfacing like So-Sheer™; Vue-Thru press cloth; bodkin; iron; and fine pins.

A STOCKING TAKES SHAPE

Cut a piece of interfacing several inches larger than the finished stocking. Pin it to the blocking board, fusible side up, and lay the template on top. Using a marking pencil or chalk, trace the template on the interfacing to mark the boundary for the ribbon weaving.

Fill the shape by pinning strips of ribbons side by side, either vertically along the stocking's length or on the diagonal, and cutting

Attaching the Cuff

Insert cuff, bottom edge down and RS out, into stocking. Align raw edges, sew, and serge. Turn cuff to outside.

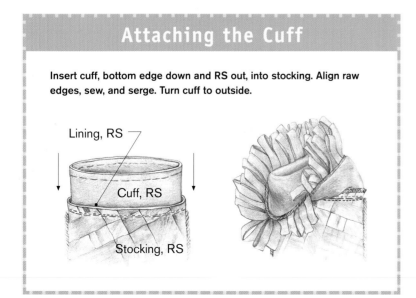

Lining, RS

Cuff, RS

Stocking, RS

them to extend 1 in. to 2 in. beyond the marked lines. Be precise, but don't worry about perfection since the ribbons will move a bit during weaving. I like to place the different ribbons randomly, varying their width, type, and color, but symmetrical placement works fine, too.

To plain-weave through the pinned ribbons, attach a bodkin to one end of a new ribbon strip and guide the bodkin over one pinned ribbon and under the next, working perpendicular to the pinned ribbons. Pin both ends of each newly woven strip to the board, adjusting all strips as needed to create a solid fabric. Press the work lightly using a press cloth, fusing the ribbon to the interfacing. Reposition the template on the weaving and retrace it. Machine-baste through all layers on the marked line, and trim the excess ribbons to a ½-in. seam allowance.

For a corded stocking edge, make piping or purchase a trim with a flange. Sew the piping or trim to the stocking front's basted line, with the cord to the inside and the raw edges aligned. Prepare a back (whether it's woven ribbon or a coordinating fabric) and cut two lining pieces.

MINIMAL ASSEMBLY REQUIRED

Stack the four layers of fabric as follows, from the bottom up: two lining pieces, right sides together; stocking front, right side up; and stocking back, right side down. Then stitch around the stocking, through all layers, leaving the top open. Reach between the front and back pieces (not the lining) to turn the stocking inside out. Baste each lining piece to the outer stocking at the top opening. Do not baste the lining pieces together.

CUFF AND TRIM

You can use vintage lace, traditional fur, or any gorgeous fabric for the cuff. To make a cuff, cut two fabric rectangles. Each one should be as wide as the top opening's cir-

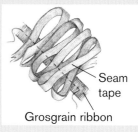
cumference, with allowances for one side seam. In addition, each rectangle should flare ½ in. wider at the bottom than at the top, so the cuff fits over the stocking. Their height should be whatever you want the finished height of the cuff to be, plus top and bottom seam allowances.

Attach a cord or fringe, if you want, to the bottom of the outer cuff. (See sidebar, "Designer Trim for Pennies" above.) With right sides together, stitch, then press open the side seam. Sew the inner cuff's side seam, then, with right sides together, join the two cuffs at the bottom. Turn right side out and baste the top edges together.

To join the cuff and stocking, pin the cuff inside the stocking, with the cuff and lining right sides together and raw edges aligned (see the drawing on the facing page). Attach a hanger loop between the cuff and lining, with the loop hanging down into the stocking. Stitch through all layers and serge or zigzag the seam's raw edges. Turn the cuff to the outside, and the stocking is ready for the holidays. ●

*Q*uick Tip

Test interfacing colors before you sew, since each may affect the color of the finished piece.

Fold a Fabric-Origami Treasure Box

*a*s the holidays approach, it's great to have a store of elegant little boxes up your gift-giving sleeve. Folded from a square of beautiful paper or from plain paper covered with fabric, these origami boxes are easy to construct in dimensions to accommodate a variety of small-sized contents, from jewelry to socks to handmade chocolates, or even cash. And the best part is that these boxes can uncomplicate your holidays! Make up a batch in a variety of fabrics to hold gifts for friends, special coworkers, teachers, and other lucky recipients.

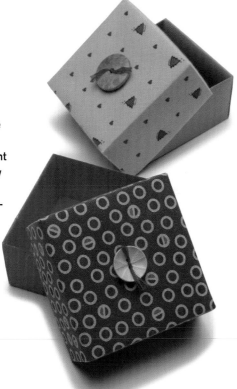

Colorful, folded-fabric gift boxes are sure to be recycled and make an elegant presentation for any small gift. A single button makes a perfect decoration for the top.

And this is a wrapping that won't be thrown away. The empty box is a treasure in itself and can quickly be adapted to a variety of other uses—perhaps as the perfect stash for buttons, earrings, business cards, tubes of sparkling beads, or sewing notions.

FABRIC OR PAPER?

The word origami comes from the Japanese *ori*, meaning "to fold," and *kami*, meaning "paper." The idea of folding paper originated in ancient China and became a truly creative art in the hands of the Japanese.

To experiment with the simple folding technique required for this box, practice making a box in paper before you begin with fabric. Ordinary computer, plain bond, or copier paper all work well for practicing and can be used for the base layer of a fabric-covered box.

To make a fabric box, you'll bond the fabric to plain paper using fusible web. The paper base stabilizes the fabric and gives it the ability to hold a creased fold.

Fabrics that work well include firmly woven cottons and medium-weight silks like dupioni. If you enjoy decorating your own fabrics, try making boxes from hand-painted silk or fabric with marbleized or rubber-stamped designs. You need only a small piece of fabric for each box (an 8½-in. square

A Unique Gift Box Begins with a Square

For 3-in.-square box, begin with 8½-in. square for top and 8¼-in. square for bottom. For other sizes, experiment using plain paper.

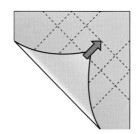

STEP 1. After fusing your fabric to the paper base, lay fabric-side down and mark center of paper square with pencil cross roughly from corner to corner (marks won't show in finished box). Fold each corner to center, crease, and unfold.

STEP 2. Fold each corner to center of farthest fold on opposite side. Crease and unfold.

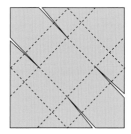

STEP 3. Cut in four places as shown, along foldlines, just to inner crease. Cuts will be on two opposite sides.

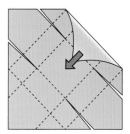

STEP 4. Fold one uncut corner to center on original crease. Fold same side again to center and crease folds. Repeat with opposite corner.

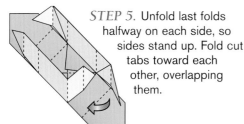

STEP 5. Unfold last folds halfway on each side, so sides stand up. Fold cut tabs toward each other, overlapping them.

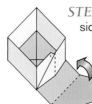

STEP 6. Fold each extended end over its tab side and down into bottom of box, creating final two box sides. Crease inside bottom with fingernail. Place dot of white glue under four corners and hold in place for moment (or, when using paper, anchor with small piece of double-sided tape).

---

makes a 3-in. box top), so your handmade fabric will go a long way.

When I'm making a batch of boxes for gifts, I often use fabric-covered paper for the box top and a coordinating paper alone for the bottom. If the box will contain chocolates or other items that might stain the box, I cut a square of clear plastic (for example, from a school-report cover) that just fits inside the bottom to protect it.

If you'd like to use paper alone for the box bottom, top, or both, choose a heavier-weight charcoal drawing paper, available at an art-supply or craft store. Or if there's a lightweight paper you want to use instead,

like rice paper, a map, a child's drawing, or wrapping paper, bond it to plain paper the same way you would fabric, as I'll explain next.

SIZING, FUSING, AND CUTTING TIPS

Cut the paper base to the exact size required for your box. In order for the box top and bottom to fit together neatly, cut the top piece about ¼ in. larger than the bottom. For example, for the 3-in. by 3-in. by 1½-in. boxes shown on the facing page, start with an 8½-in. square of paper for the top and an 8¼-in. square for the bottom.

For a smaller box, try a 6-in. square for the top and a 5¾-in. square for the bottom, which yields a box that's 2⅛ in. square and just over 1 in. high. Tiny boxes are neat, too—for example, a 4-in. square makes a 1⅜-in.-square box that's ¾ in. high. It's easy to experiment with box sizes to get one that perfectly fits its contents.

Cut the fabric and fusible web ½ in. to 1 in. larger than the paper in both directions, then trim it to size after fusing. Using an iron, fuse the web to the fabric's wrong side, following the manufacturer's directions for heat level and pressing time.

When the fabric has cooled, remove the web's protective sheet, lay the fabric right side down, cover it with the paper base and protective sheet, and fuse again, without using steam or moisture. After allowing the layers to cool once more, use a straightedge and rotary cutter to trim the fabric so that it's even with the paper base.

And now you're ready to fold, following the step-by-step instructions in the sidebar on p. 79. For neat, crisp creases, use the flat end of a burnishing tool, a bone folder, or even a plastic pen barrel to flatten each fold.

FOR A FINISHING TOUCH

Embellishing the boxes is a delight! I like to add a single new or antique button to the box top, stitching it in place with embroidery floss, metallic cord, yarn, or fine wire. The challenge is to find the right button to match the personality of each box.

To attach the button, mark a tiny X at the center of the box top. Then, holding the button in place, very gently punch a hole through the button holes and box top, using a hatpin or large needle. You can tie and cut the thread ends so that they flop on the box top, or hide them inside.

A dot of white glue will anchor the knot. In place of a button, you can tie on a single, chunky bead, or use hot-melt glue to attach a seashell, small piece of driftwood, beach glass, or other unique decoration.

For more information about origami, consult the many books available at your local library or bookstore. You can purchase books and supplies from OrigamiUSA, a not-for-profit organization dedicated to paper-folding. And origami patterns for a variety of ornaments are available from Eastwind Art (see Resources on p. 91 for contact information). Once you get started, you'll be surprised at how much fun these boxes are to make. And they're sure to make your gift-giving feel more special this year. ●

Button-Up Spreads and Throws

i have quilt-making ambitions, but my sewing workspace (and my abilities) are limited to garment-sized projects. My solution: button-apart quilts, throws, and bedspreads constructed in smaller, manageable segments and buttoned together into a larger whole. They are easier to sew and easier to wash as well. The buttons provide a functional design element, and a simple mitered hem nicely finishes the sections. I can make the individual components as small as I can comfortably work with and still have a finished piece as large as I need. I like to combine segments of compatible fabrics or piece a portion and frame it with solid-colored sections.

Any fabric sturdy enough for button closures can be used for spreads, keeping in mind the sort of wear and tear they'll receive. Prewash your fabric and any cotton or wool batting included in your project (polyester batting doesn't need prewashing).

Instructions for two different button-up styles, lined and unlined, are shown here. You can plug the concept into your own oversized designs. Spread out your ideas, and see how they shape up. ●

Cover up with an artful spread, throw, or comforter made from sections designed to button together. Smaller units are easier to sew and wash than a single, full-size quilt or throw.

How to Make a Button-Up Spread

Determine the finished overall dimensions of your project, then sketch it to scale on graph paper (or use the dimensions below). After dividing the spread into sections, draw each separately, adding laps and seam allowances. Add enough overlap for the size of your buttons. If the design is symmetrical, adjust dimensions of overlapped pieces so that each section will appear to have the same depth when buttoned (see the instructions for lined bedcover on facing page). And try shapes other than rectangles: angled and curved shapes make a puzzle game when buttoning.

Unlined Throw

Start with pieced or whole-fabric rectangles. Check to see that finished sections line up before stitching buttonhole closures.

STEP 1. Figure overall dimensions of throw, and design button sections.

STEP 2. Add 1-in. seam allowance on each section. Fuse 1-in. strip interfacing for button closure edges.

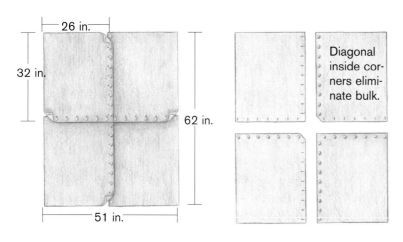

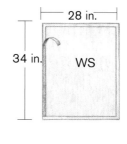

Diagonal inside corners eliminate bulk.

1-in. seam allowance for ¾-in. buttons

Serge-finish or apply seam tape to raw edges.

STEP 3. Miter corners of sections. Pinch triangle, mark, stitch turned layers together along mark. Trim and turn miter to WS. On diagonal corners, stitch across mitered edge and top, trim, turn, and press.

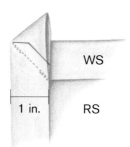

Use a postcard for instant right-angle template.

STEP 4. Topstitch all sides of each rectangle.

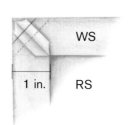

Lined Bedcover

Add ½-in. seam allowance to each top section. Line each section separately; cut lining sections 2 in. smaller in each dimension than top section. To make each panel of three-tiered spread equal size when buttoned, cut two lower sections 2 in. larger in depth to allow for underlap on each.

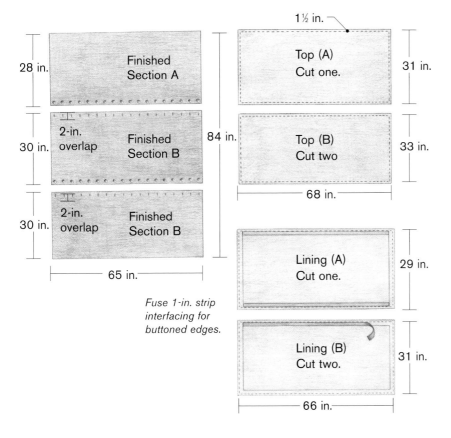

28 in. — Finished Section A

30 in. — 2-in. overlap — Finished Section B

30 in. — 2-in. overlap — Finished Section B

84 in.

65 in.

Fuse 1-in. strip interfacing for buttoned edges.

1½ in.

Top (A)
Cut one. — 31 in.

Top (B)
Cut two. — 33 in.

68 in.

Lining (A)
Cut one. — 29 in.

Lining (B)
Cut two. — 31 in.

66 in.

Miter corners of top pieces as for corners on unlined throws, leaving ½ in. unsewn.

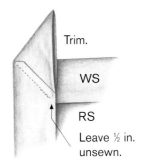

Trim.

WS

RS

Leave ½ in. unsewn.

Stitch lining to top, RSs together, turning back mitered corner from stitching path. Leave 8 in. unsewn on one edge to turn RS out.

Lining, RS

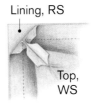

Top, WS

Needlebooks for Hand-Stitchers

Store your hand-sewing needles in a needlebook to protect them. The book can be made in any size or shape. Its soft fabric pages cushion the needles and make needle eyes and lengths easy to see. Plus, it's flat and portable. What a neat alternative to the traditional tomato pincushion.

a handy and portable place to keep your hand-sewing needles is in a needlebook, a little book with soft, fabric pages into which you insert needles and whose cover protects them. Needlebooks abounded in our great-grandmothers' sewing baskets, when hand-sewing was a part of everyday life. With the resurgence of hand-sewing, contemporary needlebooks might become heirlooms. And they're easy to make.

Needlebooks have only three basic parts—the cover, lining, and pages—but you can make myriad types of needlebooks. Possibilities include padded books or books with hard or soft covers. Covers can be decorated with your favorite embellishment on treasured or captivating fabric.

For those who love to photo-transfer, stamp, paint, and manipulate fabric, needlebooks make the perfect testing ground for new designs. On padded needlebooks, the outline of a fabric motif can be quilt-stitched. Scraps of trims and cordings can find a home in a needlebook.

Closures can run the creative spectrum, and pockets are easy to add for holding scissors or needles that come in packets. Needlebooks can be any shape and size, and can be designed to accommodate any unusual needles, such as the extra-long needles that are used by milliners, dollmakers, and stitchers of Brazilian embroidery.

If you need ideas, you can find them in books on journal-making and origami. Whatever the

A needlebook has three basic parts: a cover, lining, and fabric pages. Here are directions for making three types of books.

Pocketed Needlebook

Needlebooks can be any size: These directions make a 5-in. by 8-in. book. The pockets hold packages of both hand and machine needles.

STEP 1. Cut needle pages 7½ in. square, pink edges, and set aside.

STEP 2. Cut lining fabric 19½ in. by 8½ in. Fold each short end of lining to inside 4½ in. from raw edge. Fold again, to outside, matching raw edge to first fold, and stitch pockets as shown through three layers.

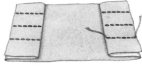

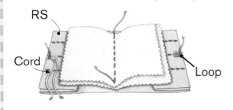

RS

Cord

Loop

STEP 3. Using center-pocket stitching as placement guide, sew cord and cord loop to lining's WS. Stitch needle pages to lining at center.

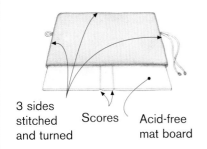

3 sides stitched and turned   Scores   Acid-free mat board

STEP 4. Cut cover fabric 8½ in. by 10½ in. with RSs together, stitch cover to lining on sides and top with ¼-in. seam allowances. Turn. Insert 8-in. by 10-in. acid-free mat board, scored as shown. Turn under raw edges of fabric opening, whipstitch closed.

Padded Needlebook

Here's a needlebook that can be quilted. The lining is two padded squares stitched to the cover and spine.

STEP 1. To make a finished, 3¾-in.-square padded needlebook, cut the following:

- Fabric cover, 8½ in. by 4¾ in.

- Cover padding (batting), 7½ in. by 3¾ in.

- For lining, two 3⅛-in. squares of mat board and padding, and two each 4⅛-in.-square pieces of lining fabric.

- Spine fabric, 4¼ in. by 2 in.

STEP 2. Glue padding to mat board, let dry. Wrap each lining square around layers, folding and gluing seam allowances to inside.

STEP 3. Center and lightly sew padding to cover's WS, turning seam allowances to inside and mitering corners. Quilt.

STEP 4. Center 27-in. ribbon-tie closure on WS of cover, parallel to long edges.

STEP 5. Fold under ½-in. seam allowances at ends of spine; set aside. Cut linen pages 7 in. by 3¼ in.; finish edges with blanket stitch.

STEP 6. Center pages on spine and stitch through all layers. Whipstitch spine to cover as shown.

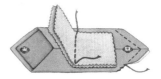

WS

WS

STEP 7. WSs together, hand-stitch padded squares to inside of cover.

Necktie Needlebook

Construction of this needlebook is quick, since the lining, interfacing, and finishing are already completed in the necktie. (See bottom photo p. 86.)

STEP 1. Cut 9½ in. off tie's narrow end. Fold under ½-in. seam allowances on outer and lining fabric; slipstitch closed to match first point. Stitch top-center edges closed for 1 in.

STEP 2. Cut 9½ in. off tie's wide end for needlebook's cover. Fold ½-in. seam allowances to inside; slipstitch closed to match point.

STEP 3. Use interfacing from another tie for pages. Cut pages 6 in. by 2½ in., pink edges, stitch to cover as shown. If desired, attach with decorative machine stitch (will show on cover's RS).

STEP 4. Hand-stitch narrow section to wide section at center fold. On front, stitch narrow sections' outer edges 1 in. from top. Add snap or other closure.

design of your needle-
book, it's certain
to be an individual
and personal place
to keep a hand-sewer's
basic tools. To get
started, why not try one
of my three favorite
needlebook designs.

FABRIC FOR MAKING NEEDLEBOOKS

For a needlebook's pages,
soft linen, flannel, or woven
nonfusible interfacings are good
choices. Generally, any woven fabric is
suitable, but don't use dyed polyester felts
for the book's leaves—these attract moisture
and can cause needles to rust.

The cover of your needlebook can be
made from woven fabrics of all sorts, from
luxurious brocades, decorator fabric, remnants, strips of an unusual ribbon sewn together, or even a recycled necktie. Leather is
an option, and Ultrasuede is another good
choice.

With regard to a lining for your needlebook's cover, again use any woven fabric,
or simply self-line the interior. If you are
making a padded needlebook, it's a good
idea to use a tightly
woven fabric to prevent the
batting fibers from "bearding"—that is,
working their way through the fabric.

If the fabrics for the cover, padding, and
lining combine to make a thick cover, you
will need to include a spine to compensate for
the added bulk (see instructions for Pocketed
and Padded Needlebooks on p. 85).

So why not give your hand-sewing needles luxury accommodations, create an heirloom, and have fun all at the same time by
making a special, unique, and functional
needlebook? ●

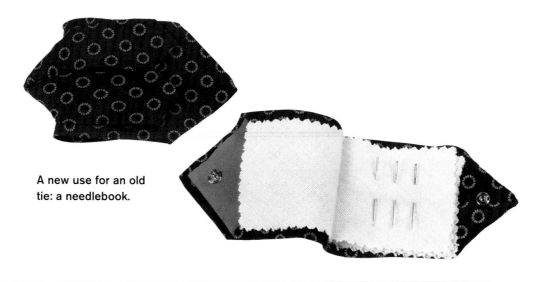

A new use for an old tie: a needlebook.

Customized Hangers

*t*he idea for a custom-shaped, padded hanger was born when I finished a coat that had relatively shallow shoulders. As we all know, a garment needs to hang properly from the shoulders to keep its shape when stored. Hung on a coat hanger, my coat sprouted vertical folds around the armhole. On a dress hanger, folds appeared around the neckline. No good.

I needed to make a special hanger, so I devised the black velvet hanger shown above, which mates perfectly with my shallow-shouldered coat. And the two padded, shirred, ribboned, and embellished hangers shown at right have elements that are meaningful to the garments that rest upon them now.

Now I'm hooked on making a personalized hanger as the final task for all my sewing projects. In addition to having a hanger that fits the garment perfectly, there's the added bonus of incorporating embellishments, such as labels, ribbons, and leftover garment fabric on the hanger. I've found that stretch fabric is slightly easier to use for a hanger than woven fabric, which may take a few fittings to get a taut, smooth surface.

All in all, these hangers provide an easy, satisfying show of respect for the care and labor that's gone into sewing the garments themselves. The drawings on p. 88 show how to construct the coat hanger pictured above. For the hangers in the photo at right,

begin with ready-made, padded dress hangers and cover them with fabric. Both covers are made by sewing tubes, each closed at one end, that slip over the ends of the hanger, meet at the hook, and get slipstitched together. Each tube is made of a bottom section that's half the hanger's length and a top section its full length, which, when gathered, produces the shirred effect you see. The top hanger has buttons sewn at each end to keep spaghetti straps from slipping off. These hangers are quick and fun to make and reflect details from each outfit. Now garments can look as good on the hanger as they do on the body. ●

Padded dress hangers don't require the contouring needed for a coat. They're just plain fun to make and embellish.

The structure of a coat needs a three-dimensionally shaped hanger. The black velvet hanger on p. 87 incorporates the exact shoulder slope and depth needed to fill out the shaping of the coat it was made for.

STEP 1. On cardboard, trace both shoulder slopes of coat. Mark hanger's height (minus hook) and depth, as shown. Trace mirror image of shoulder slopes below hanger-depth lines. Cut out traced shape. Score hanger-depth lines, fold up around suit hanger. Cut top sections, matching slopes and hanger depth to cardboard.

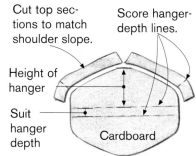

Cut top sections to match shoulder slope.

Score hanger-depth lines.

Height of hanger

Suit hanger depth

Cardboard

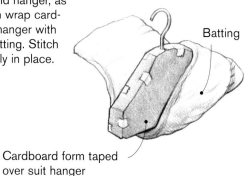

Cardboard

Coat's actual slope

Coat

Original suit hanger

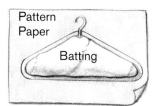

Suit hanger depth

STEP 2. Tape cardboard pieces around hanger, as shown. Then wrap cardboard-form hanger with polyester batting. Stitch ends securely in place.

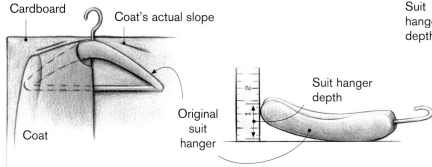

Batting

Cardboard form taped over suit hanger

STEP 3. To draft pattern for hanger cover, trace around hanger unit on paper, adding half hanger depth plus ⅜-in. seam allowance all around. If using stretch fabric, do not add seam allowance. Cut pattern twice from fabric.

Pattern Paper

Batting

STEP 4. Make tube of fabric to snugly cover hanger hook. Slip fabric tube over hook; slipstitch bottom end to batting.

STEP 5. Sew cover fabric, RSs together, on top and sides, leaving small opening for hook, and larger opening on underside for inserting hanger.

STEP 6. Turn cover to RS out, put on hanger, adjust seam allowances if needed. When snug, slipstitch bottom edge closed. Decorate hanger with rosettes, labels, etc.

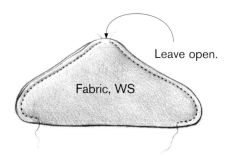

Leave open.

Fabric, WS

Pincushions with Personality

ollecting miniature dress forms, both old and contemporary, has become a minor passion of mine— I love them for their charming variations in size and shape, the materials they're made from (wood, wire, and muslin), and their undeniable character. I wonder about the sewers who created them: Were they students practicing making the real thing in the days when poured or taped forms hadn't been thought of? Or were they sewers making them just for fun?

I had a great deal of fun when I made a miniature dress form for myself to serve as a pincushion in my much-too-serious studio. I admit I got carried away—the plump shapes are an irresistible delight to create and embellish, as I've done with the "Tomato Lady" (above) and the "Home Décor Lady" (below). I also like to leave them plain, resembling

their grown-up counterparts. These diminutive dress forms seem to take on a life of their own, and they keep me company during those long stretches of solitary sewing.

I've provided a pattern and construction steps for making your own miniature dress form, but try different sizes and shapes, which are easily made by redrawing the pattern. Try creating one that's short and wide, an hourglass ideal, or one that reminds you of Aunt Mabel.

The red arrows in the pattern drawings show where you can enlarge, reduce, reshape, or lengthen the pattern pieces for a differently sized form. It's intentional that I haven't told you exactly how much to change these dimensions: Take some guesses and see what sews up. In the process, you could learn something about full-size alterations or fitting by fooling around with the miniature pattern. Follow only one rule in resizing the dress form: Make changes on the seamlines, then add new seam allowances. Check that seam measurements match in length (unless you want to try some darting or easing), and remember that incremental changes to any pattern with multiple vertical seams make a huge difference when added up. And, my final suggestion: have fun! ●

The "Home Décor Lady" (bottom left) and the "Tomato Lady" (top left) are pincushions with presence.

Muslin works well as a dress-form fabric, since it's stable and resembles a full-size form. Stenciled lettering adds an authentic touch.

How to Make a Dress-Form Pincushion

1. PREPARATION. If appropriate, fuse interfacing to back of lightweight, loosely woven, or transparent fabric. Cut out pattern pieces, maintaining grainlines and adding ¼-in. seam allowances. Transfer shoulder notches.

2. BODICE. Note: It's easier to sew necks and armholes by hand rather than machine. Sew neckband CF seam. Then, matching notches, stitch neck top to neckband. Sew princess seams on backs and fronts. Press seams open (and all seams that follow as soon as each is sewn). Next, sew bodice CF seam, then darts and, lastly, shoulder seams. Machine staystitch (follow seamline with tiny stitches) neckline and armholes. Sew bodice CB seam. Hand-backstitch neckband to bodice, matching notches to shoulder seam. Sew side seams, then sew armhole seams.

3. SKIRT. Sew vertical seams in skirt: princess seams, CF, CB, and side seams. Now sew skirt to bodice at waist. Finally, staystitch ¼ in. from bottom edge. Turn under along stitches. Press.

4. BASE. Cut stiff paper, poster board, oaktag, or thin plastic slightly smaller than the base pattern's size. Insert base between two layers of base fabric. Baste ¼ in. from outer edge.

5. STUFFING AND EMBELLISH-MENT. Pack Fiberfill into form, firmly filling out all curves. Handstitch base to form, matching notches. Add more Fiberfill as you stitch if needed. Handstitch base closed. Embellish to suit personality that has emerged from your miniature dress form.

These miniature dress forms acquire their own personality and spark creativity in their makers. Use these pattern pieces for your first form, then try varying them using the "change-her-body-shape" arrows (shown in red below) as guides if needed.

Enlarge patterns, then cut two of each from your fabric, reversing one. Cut one neckband and one neck top.

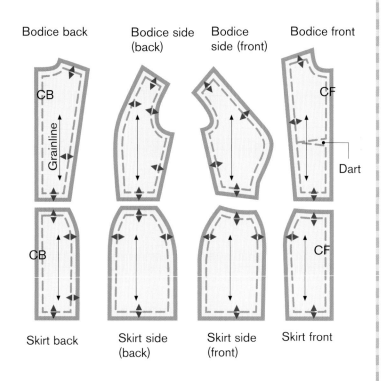

Bodice back · Bodice side (back) · Bodice side (front) · Bodice front

CB · Grainline · CF · Dart

CB · CF

Skirt back · Skirt side (back) · Skirt side (front) · Skirt front

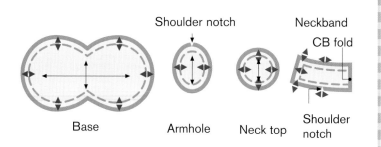

Shoulder notch · Neckband · CB fold

Base · Armhole · Neck top · Shoulder notch

Resources

Artemis, Inc.
179 High St.
South Portland, ME 04106
(888) 233-5187
www.artemisinc.com
Bias-cut silk ribbon

Atlanta Thread and Supply
695 Red Oak Rd.
Stockbridge, GA 30281
(800) 847-1001
www.atlantathread.com
Batting

B & J Fabrics
263 W. 40th St.
New York, NY 10018
(212) 354-8150
Rayon/silk velvet

Baer Fabrics
515 E. Market St.
Louisville, KY 40202
(800) 769-7778
Variety of pillow forms

Banksville Fabrics
115 New Canaan Ave.
Norwalk, CT 06850
(203) 846-1333
Rayon/silk velvet

Bead Warehouse
PO Box 8550
Burlington, VT 05402
(802) 658-0013
Seed and crystal beads

Bernadine's Needle Art
P.O. Box 41
Arthur, IL 61911
(217) 543-2996
www.bernadinesneedleart.com
Russian needlepunch embroidery
supplies

The Button Emporium
914 S.W. 11th Ave.
Portland, OR 97205
(503) 228-6372
www.buttonemporium.com
French and Japanese organdy ribbon,
solid and variegated

The Button Shoppe
4744 Oakfield Circle
Carmichael, CA 95608
(916) 488-5350
(888) 254-6078
www.buttonshoppe.com
Buckles

The Clay Factory of Escondido
PO Box 460598
Escondido, CA 92046-0598
(800) 243-3466
www.clayfactoryinc.com
Pasta machine, glue

Designer Fabrics
1360 Queen St. W.
Toronto, ON M6K 1L7
Canada
(416) 531-2810
www.designerfabrics.com
Trims and braiding supplies, including
soutache

Dick Blick
PO Box 1267
Galesburg, IL 61402
(800) 828-4548
www.dickblick.com
Papers for gift boxes

Down Decor
1910 South St.
Cincinnati, OH 45204
(800) 792-DOWN
Feather/down pillow forms

Edinburgh Imports
PO Box 340
Newbury Park, CA 91319-0340
(800) 334-6274
www.edinburgh.com
Wool felt

Eastwind Art
PO Box 811
Sebastopol, CA 95473
(707) 829-3536
www.eastwindart.com
Origami patterns and supplies

Elsie's Exquisiques
7225 Lenox Ave.
Riverside, CA 92504
(800) 742-7455
Japanese organdy ribbon; silk
soutache in 12 colors

Fanny's Fabrics
7130 Fisher Rd. SE
Calgary, AB T2H 0W3
Canada
(800) 481-9867
Variety of pillow forms

General Bead
317 National City Blvd.
National City, CA 91950-1110
(619) 336-0100
Beading thread

Ginsco Trims
242 W. 38th St.
New York, NY 10018
(800) 929-2529
www.ginstrim.com
Soutache and president's braid in a
wide range of colors

A Great Notion Sewing Supply
101-5630 Landmark Way
Surrey, BC V3S 7H1
Canada
(604) 533-2891
www.agreatnotion.com
Designer Tacky Glue, fusible web,
and Hera markers

Hancock's of Paducah
3841 Hinkleville Rd.
Paducah, KY 42001
(800) 845-8723
www.hancocks-paducah.com
Variety of pillow forms

Hot Potatoes
209 10th Ave. S.
Suite 311
Nashville, TN 37203
(615) 269-8002
Stamp supplies

Magic Cabin Dolls
1950 Waldorf N.W.
Grand Rapids, MI 49550-7000
(888) 623-6557
www.magiccabin.com
Wool felt

Mindy's Needlepoint Factory
296 E. 5th Ave.
Eugene, OR 97401
(541) 344-7132
www.mindysneedlepoint.com
Books and supplies for silk-ribbon and
Brazilian embroidery

Debra Moises
244 W. 74th St.
Suite 9A
New York, NY 10023
Send an SASE for information on
variegated ribbon Ombre scarf and
Mirage shawl kits, prices, and ordering

Mokuba
577 Queen St. W.
Toronto, ON M5V2B6
Canada
(416) 504-5358
www.festivegiftwrap.com
Japanese organdy ribbon; sample
cards $2.50 (Canadian) each

Nancy's Notions
333 Beichl Ave.
PO Box 683
Beaver Dam, WI 53916-0683
(800) 833-0690
www.nancysnotions.com
Designer Tacky Glue, Fiber-Etch,
fusible web, Hera markers, rotary
cutter

National Nonwovens
PO Box 150
Easthampton, MA 01027
(800) 333-3469
www.nationalnonwovens.com
Wool felt

The Ohio Hempery
PO Box 18
Guysville, OH 45735
(800) 289-4367
www.hempery.com
Hemp cord and braid

Oregon Tailor Supply
PO Box 42284
Portland, OR 97242
(800) 678-2457
www.oregontailor.com
Dressmaker's seam tape in small
quantities; glazed cotton thread

OrigamiUSA
15 W. 77th St.
New York, NY 10024
(212) 769-5635
www.origami-usa.org
Origami books and supplies

Personal Stamp Exchange
Sierra Enterprises
P.O. Box 5325
Petaluma, CA 94955
(800) 782-6748
www.psxdesign.com
Stamp supplies

Purrfection Artistic Wearables
19618 Canyon Dr.
Granite Falls, WA 98252
(800) 691-4293
www.purrfection.com
Stamp supplies

Quilters' Resource, Inc.
PO Box 148850
Chicago, IL 60614
(800) 676-6543
www.quiltersresource.com
Silk and silk-satin ribbon, bias-cut ribbon, textured rayon ribbon, and braids

Renaissance Buttons
Box 130
Oregon House, CA 95962
(530) 692-1663
www.renaissancebuttons.com
New and vintage buckles and buttons

Renaissance Ribbons
PO Box 699
Oregon House, CA 95962
(530) 692-0842
www.renaissanceribbons.com
Braids

Ribbon Connections, Inc.
2971 Teagarden St.
San Leandro, CA 94577
(510) 614-1825
www.ribbonconnections.com
Silk-satin ribbon

The Ribbonerie
191 Potrero Ave.
San Francisco, CA 94103
(415) 626-6184
www.theribbonerie.com
Trims, including metallic soutache

The Ribbonry
119 Louisiana Ave.
Perrysburg, OH 43551
(419) 872-0073
www.ribbonry.com
French and Japanese organdy ribbon,
solid and variegated

Rings & Things
P.O. Box 450
Spokane, WA 99210
(800)366-2156
www.rings-things.com
Pin backs

Sax Arts & Crafts
PO Box 510710
New Berlin, WI 53151
(800) 558-6696
www.saxarts.com
Acrylic roller, needle tool, E6000 glue

Silkpaint Corp.
PO Box 18-TH
Waldron, MO 64092
(816) 891-7774
www.silkpaint.com
Fiber-Etch; P4 Thickener

Thai Silks
252 State St.
Los Altos, CA 94022
(800) 722-7455
www.thaisilks.com
Rayon/silk velvet; swatches available

Tinsel Trading Co.
47 W. 38th St.
New York, NY 10018
(212) 768-8823
www.tinseltrading.com
Braid, fringe, new and vintage trims,
tassels

Vogue Fabrics
718 Main St.
Evanston, IL 60202
(847) 864-9600
www.myvoguefabrics.com
Free melton-cloth swatches and fine
monofilament thread

Wee Folk Creations
18476 Natchez Ave.
Prior Lake, MN 55372
(888) 933-3655
www.weefolk.com
Brush-on lacquer, metallic powders,
button shanks

Credits

The articles compiled in this book appeared in the following issues of *Threads*.

p. 6: "The Saturn Hatpin" by Ingrid Fraley, on-line article. Photos by Judi Rutz, © The Taunton Press, Inc. Illustrations by Christine Erikson.

p. 8: "From Buttons to Bracelets" by Marlene O'Tousa, issue 79. Photos by Judi Rutz, © The Taunton Press, Inc. Illustrations by Christine Erikson.

p. 11: "Patchwork Puzzle Pins" by Therese M. Inverso, issue 73. Photos © Sloan Howard.

p. 14: "Fabric Cuff Bracelets" by Roxy White, issue 89. Photos © Sloan Howard.

p. 16: "Old-World Treasures: Clay Buttons and Jewelry" (originally " 'Clay' Buttons and Jewelry—Ancient or Modern?") by Annie Coan, issue 66. Photos by Karen Morris, © The Taunton Press, Inc.

p. 18: "Gorgeous Beaded Buttons: Make Just One or a Set" by Jane Conlon, issue 81. Photos © Sloan Howard. Illustrations by Christine Erikson.

p. 22: "Stamped Fabric Is Only the Beginning" by Mary Jo Hiney, on-line article. Photos by Sloan Howard, © The Taunton Press, Inc.

p. 24: "Your Very Own Dévoré Velvet" (originally "Your Very Own Cut Velvet") by Karen Morris, issue 72. Photos by Scott Phillips, © The Taunton Press, Inc. Illustrations by Carla Ruzicka.

p. 27: "Dimensional Embroidery" by Wanda Gayer, issue 63. Photos by Scott Phillips, © The Taunton Press, Inc.

p. 30: "Take the Ribbon Road" by Mary Jo Hiney, issue 92. Photos © Sloan Howard.

p. 34: "Call 'em Irresistible— Beads and Tulle" by Debra Blum and Moises Diaz, issue 74. Photos by Scott Phillips, © The Taunton Press, Inc. Illustrations by Robert LaPointe.

p. 37: "Gossamer Ribbon-Work Scarves" by Debra Blum and Moises Diaz, issue 80. Photos by Scott Phillips, © The Taunton Press, Inc. Illustrations by Kathy Bray.

p. 40: "Stitch an Easy Bra-Slip" by Connie Long, issue 69. Photos by Scott Phillips, © The Taunton Press, Inc. Illustrations by Carla Ruzicka.

p. 42: "Seashells to Wear" by Judy Atwell, issue 71. Photos by Scott Phillips, © The Taunton Press, Inc. Illustrations by Carla Ruzicka.

p. 44: "Easy Braided Belts" by Nancy Nehring, issue 83. Photos by Sloan Howard, © The Taunton Press, Inc. Illustrations by Kathy Bray.

p. 48: "Two Sew-Easy Scarves" (originally "The Easiest Cowl-Neck Scarf") by Karen Morris, issue 60. Photos by Boyd Hagen, © The Taunton Press, Inc.

p. 50: "Wrap Yourself in Soutache" by Karen Morris, issue 75. Photos by Scott Phillips, © The Taunton Press, Inc. Illustrations by Kathy Bray.

p. 52: "Variations on a Shrug" by Laura White, issue 85. Photos © Jack Deutsch. Sketches by Lamont O'Neal. Illustrations by Karen Meyer.

p. 55: "Stitch a Pie Bag" by Laura White, issue 87. Photos © Sloan Howard. Illustrations by Christine Erikson.

p. 58: "Overstitched Bags and Portfolios" by Susan B. Allen, issue 65. Photos by Scott Phillips, © The Taunton Press, Inc. Illustrations by Frank Habbas.

p. 60: "The Simplest Summer Skirt" by Karen Morris, issue 77. Photos by Scott Phillips, © The Taunton Press, Inc.

p. 64: "Embroidered Felt Trivets" by Mary Jo Hiney, issue 88. Photos © Sloan Howard. Illustrations by Karen Meyer.

p. 67: "Pillow and Pyramid Gift Boxes" by Jane Conlon, issue 67. Photos by Scott Phillips, © The Taunton Press, Inc. Illustrations by Carla Ruzicka.

p. 70: "A Pillow from Neckties" by Shirley Botsford, issue 78. Photos by Scott Phillips, © The Taunton Press, Inc. Illustrations by Robert LaPointe.

p. 72: "Great Pillows 1,2,3" by Linda Lee, issue 76. Photos by Scott Phillips, © The Taunton Press, Inc. Illustrations by Kim Jaeckel.

p. 76: "Ribbonwork Holiday Stocking" by Linda Lee, issue 68. Photos by Scott Phillips, © The Taunton Press, Inc. Illustrations by Carla Ruzicka.

p. 78: "Fold a Fabric-Origami Treasure Box" by Louise LoPinto Hutchison, issue 79. Photos by Sloan Howard, © The Taunton Press, Inc. Illustrations by Karen Meyer adapted from *Origami Ornaments* by Eastwind Art.

p. 81: "Button-Up Spreads and Throws" by Denise Alborn, issue 90. Photos by Sloan Howard, © The Taunton Press, Inc. Illustrations by Eugene Marino II.

p. 84: "Needlebooks for Hand-Stitchers" by Christine M. Anderson, issue 93. Photos by Sloan Howard, © The Taunton Press, Inc. Illustrations by Christine Erikson.

p. 87: "Customized Hangers" by Anna Mazur, issue 94. Photos by Sloan Howard, © The Taunton Press, Inc. Illustrations by Bob LaPointe.

p. 89: "Pincushions with Personality" by Sally McCann, issue 95. Photos by Sloan Howard, © The Taunton Press, Inc. Illustrations by Linda Boston.

Front matter photo credits

p. i: Sloan Howard, © The Taunton Press, Inc.

p. iv: (top left) Karen Morris, © The Taunton Press, Inc.

p. iv: (top right) Sloan Howard, © The Taunton Press, Inc.

p. iv: (bottom left) Judi Rutz, © The Taunton Press, Inc.

p. iv: (bottom right) Scott Phillips, © The Taunton Press, Inc.

p. 1: (top left and top right) Scott Phillips, © The Taunton Press, Inc.

p. 1: (bottom) Sloan Howard, © The Taunton Press, Inc.

Section openers photo credits

p. 4: Sloan Howard, © Sloan Howard

p. 5: Sloan Howard, © Sloan Howard

pp. 20, 21, 32, 33, 62: Scott Phillips © The Taunton Press, Inc.

p. 63: Sloan Howard, © The Taunton Press, Inc.